Beyond the Plan:

The Transformation of Personal Space in Housing

The path to
homeownership
begins
@ your library™

www.ala.org/rusa/WellsFargo

ALA American Library Association · WELLS FARGO | HOME MORTGAGE

By Stephen Willats

First published in Great Britain in 2001 by
WILEY-ACADEMY

Adivision of
JOHN WILEY & SONS
Baffins Lane
Chichester
West Sussex PO19 1UD

ISBN: 0-471-49561-1

Other Wiley Editorial offices:
New York, Weinheim, Brisbane, Singapore, Toronto.

Designed and typeset by Katy Hepburn.
Printed and bound in Italy.

Contents

'A Walk Along the Balcony'. February/March 1992.
Five-panel work. Each panel 50 cm x 32 cm. Photographic prints,
photographic dye, acrylic paint, Letraset text on card.

Beyond the plan
Introduction

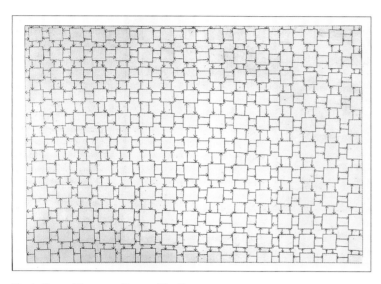

Fig. 1 *Above: 'Homeostat Drawing No. 1', 1969. 71.12 cm wide x 55.88 cm high. Pencil on paper. This drawing represented an important model in my work as it depicted a social state where all nodes are equal and information is accessible to all within a one layer network.*

Fig. 2 *Right: A basic model for a homeostatic self-organising system, showing total coupling between elements A, B, C, D. Elements can achieve an Effector/Affector condition as a result of the total coupling.*

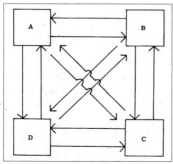

Going 'beyond the plan' has been central to my work as an artist since the early 1960s. The plan in 'beyond the plan' refers to someone else's plans that have been made on my behalf, so perhaps it is no surprise that I found in architecture, in the planned environments of housing estates, of office blocks, shopping centres etc., that emerged as icons of a 'new reality' in the 1960s, a context for the development of the language and meaning in my work. The relationship between the shaping of the physical world, and an ideological view of that world, also meant that the planned estate environments were highly polemical, even controversial realms for me to explore. For in my work the idea of the plan, the determinism inherent in institutional planning, has been juxtaposed with the concept of self-organisation expressed as the ability of a system to change and determine its own relationships between the elements that comprise its various parts. I saw that self-organisation coupled with the ability to transform — to see that one thing could be another, both in meaning and function — were fundamental components of creative behaviour. This was in the light of my exposure to models of communication and decision making in the new emerging spirit of the times. These were dynamic one layer networks of exchange, that were shaping the vision of the future through philosophical disciplines such as Cybernetics, Information Theory and Learning Theory.[1]

What I saw as potentially so important about these models of society was that there was no fixed hierarchy, that within the network all 'nodes' were equal (Figs. 1 and 2). Communication was through a two way exchange not just via the determinism of a one way transmission, so that there was the inherent possibility of a 'question' arising between anyone in the network, which immediately implies an active contributory state between nodes, a state conducive to self-organisation (Fig. 3). Exposure to the models led to an important realisation in my practice, for I saw that the artist was in an interpersonal network with the audience, and was in fact dependent upon it, and that within this network the audience was as important to it as the artist.[2] As a consequence, quite different and enlarged realms of meaning could be opened up between the artist and audience, for the latter could now participate in the construction of the meaning. Following on from this, and developed further in the late 1960s and early 1970s, was the basic recognition that the work of art's existence and meaning are not the product of any one person, that in reality sole authorship does not exist but is an artificial construction made by a culture built on a society founded upon authoritative hierarchies. I felt then in the early 1960s and even more today that 'art' was dependent on society, on beliefs, relationships, attitudes, norms and conventions between people. Moreover that 'art' and creative expression in general were contextual to those realms of relationships in which they existed and were perceived to have a function. During 1962/63 I drew up a series of manifestos which attempted to map out an approach to a cultural future that recognised the random and multichannel nature of reality, and the inherent role of self-organisation in creating perceptual order. At this moment I could not help but become aware of the enormous role modern buildings were taking on in shaping our perception of the future. These buildings were symbols of the 'new world' to come; they gave a certainty to what could be expected. Consequently one of my manifestos centred on the position of the architect (Fig. 4).

While, like so many others, I was excited by the symbolism of modern building, by the outface of its mass and presence in the city, I was also becoming aware of another aspect to these buildings, a dark side, as reflected in the hidden, segmented structure of their interiors. That within the block, the box-like slab or tower, were many identical

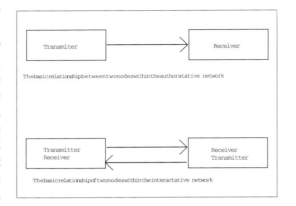

The basic relationship between two nodes within the authoratative network

The basic relationship of two nodes within the interactative network

Fig. 5 *'Organic Exercise No. 2. Series Two' (Tower Block Study), August 1962. 53.34cm x 78.74cm. Ink on paper.*

Opposite top:
Fig. 3 *The basic relationship between two nodes within the authoritative network. The basic relationship of two nodes within the interactive network.*
Opposite below:
Fig. 4 *One of a series of self published manifestos that were created by typing with several sheets of carbon paper between the papers. They were given out at openings of exhibitions, distributed to other artists.*

box-like interiors containing many different lives and that their individual richness was not recognised in the repetitive, reductive, unit based design that was the building's outface. Also there was an internal conflict between the monumental outface of these modern buildings and the communication driven culture towards which they were supposed to be pointing the way. Until the late 1960s, this remained more of an observation (though the idea of a segmented interior did influence a series of drawings; see Fig. 5), but then the polemic between outside and inside came to be an important concern as a result of an experimental artwork I initiated in Nottingham titled 'Man From The Twenty First Century'.

'Man From The Twenty First Century' was undertaken through the Department of Fine Art at Trent Polytechnic during 1969/70 which I initiated and then developed with students. The work's intentions and procedures have been documented and discussed elsewhere,[3] but suffice it to say here that the idea was to demonstrate that the artist could work within the infrastructure of society, and using relevant methodologies could actively involve audiences quite outside those of traditional gallery visiting groups. One of the objectives of this particular work was to build a meta language between two quite separated communities, separated geographically, economically and socially. The idea behind building the meta language was to facilitate communication between the two groups, enabling each then to construct a model of the other, and communicate it to the other group, and in the process reveal more about themselves to each other. One of the two areas, Hyson Green, was a very 'working class' inner city neighbourhood of cobbled streets and terraces; the other, Bramcote Hills, was then a just completed young-executive-style suburban development. Working with the students I sought to build the meta language up from the existing languages present in the two neighbourhoods. Consequently, working with a door-to-door questionnaire (Fig. 6) and a mass photographic documentation, a research process was undertaken to uncover signs and symbols that would have a common meaning throughout a neighbourhood. What was revealed immediately, and has had a fundamental influence on the work of this book, was the role of objects placed in the front window and the expressive personalisation of the facade, front doors, brickwork etc.

At Bramcote Hills the picture window took on an overt role as a stage for personal display. The passer-by was attracted to look into the living room, usually via a display of objects placed in the window that would convey a desired message about the occupants, and quite often this would reinforce the bright, contemporary, forward-looking message of the building itself. At the time of the project, the houses of Bramcote Hills had just been completed, but already residents were customising them, layering the outside with individual elements such as Greek pillars, trelliswork, or positioning status symbols such as a speed boat or a caravan in the driveway. The doors, as supplied when new, were also frequently changed to express the difference between residents, but still these changes were within a permissible bandwidth for the expression of individuality.

Similarly, but in quite a different way, at Hyson Green the front living-room window also played an important role, but here objects, often potted plants, seemed to have the role of keeping you out, of stopping you from looking in, while at the same time confirming that the occupant 'belonged' to the neighbourhood. Front doors were predominately painted in a specific dark green, although some were replaced in colours and designs which expressed the non-acceptance of the general atmosphere of the surroundings. At Hyson Green especially I was struck how different messages seemed to coexist, even though they appear to go in different directions. While at first sight both project areas could be thought of as a symbolic jungle, this was far from the truth, for the adaptations and self expression were articulated within a bandwidth of what was acceptable, especially at Bramcote Hills; it was as if a topology had been set within which self expression could occur. As might be expected at Bramcote Hills, expression was generally forward looking, although there were

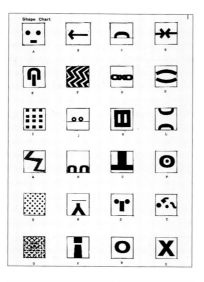

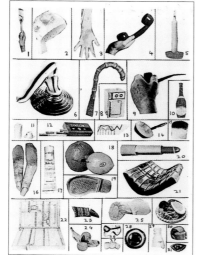

Fig. 6 'Man From The Twenty-First Century', 1971. A4 pages of montages from the doorstep questionnaire.

occasional displays that denoted the past, perhaps reminders of where people originally came from. But at the long established neighbourhood of Hyson Green, the variety of expression on the facade of the building had become quite complex over time, and many of the adaptations to what were almost identical buildings became a denial of the past, an attempt to get away from the now defunct history of the area. What struck me as fundamentally important at the time, was that standardised architectural units had been personalised by the occupants, and that in walking down the street visible evidence of this implicitly and explicitly effected your perception of them. In our work 'Man From The Twenty First Century', in each project area, patterns were detected that formed a restricted code,[4] in the use of colours, on the facade and in the front garden adornments, and in window objects. The particular association people attached to items, especially in the context of their particular neighbourhood, facilitated their representation in the meta language.

Several years later when, in the early 1970s, I formulated the strategies underpinning the West London Social Resource Project[5] (Fig. 7) and the Edinburgh Social Model Construction Project,[6] I actively sought out the languages that were restricted to the particular context in which the audience lived in order to build the language of those works. I saw that the special meaning for people that these restricted codes already had meant they could connect to realms of association immediately, and hence the employment of these codes in the works would create a ready point of access into the ideas presented. Both these works, while having differences in form and objectives, took the idea of an artwork operating as a time-based evolving communication strategy. This was grounded in interaction and exchange directly into the living environment and behaviours of the participants. The works invited people to transform the way in which those environments and behaviours were perceived. The idea of using the audience's language was a pragmatic strategy as the works engaged people to whom attention to art was a low priority, people who were right outside the institutional realm of art and its

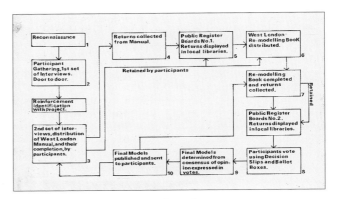

Fig. 7 *Flow chart of project events that took place over nine months in 1972.*

preoccupations. So to gain these people's active involvement the work would have to address what was already meaningful for them, and do so in their existing language.

Even before the structure of the West London Social Resource Project or the Edinburgh Social Model Construction Project was devised I identified the small neighbourhoods called Project Areas, from which people would be invited to participate, and then embarked on research reconnaissance of the areas to document the neighbourhood language (Fig. 8).

I looked at the relationship between public, institutional signs and the individual displays made by residents, photographing identifiable

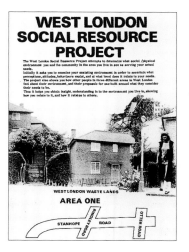

Fig. 8 *The four project area leaflets showing recognisable signs and objects from each project area. Greenford, Osterley, Hanwell and Harrow Project Areas.*

items from the various Project Areas (Fig. 9) which people living in those areas would either actually recognise as belonging or see as similar to what they themselves possessed. This representation of familiarity increased the relevance of the work, and the motivation to participate in an activity which must have been seen by residents as varying considerably from what they expected of an artwork.

The main participatory device of these works was the 'question' presented in relation to problem situations constructed using texts and photographs of the items documented during my reconnaissance of the Project Areas. Both works were essentially in two parts, the first part was descriptive and centred on externalising to individuals and the community how they saw things as they already existed. Participants responded to Problem Situations presented in a publication, book or folder such as 'The West London Manual', or on Response Sheets (Fig. 10) as in the case of the Edinburgh project, recording writings, diagrams and drawings that could be displayed later on a public register (Fig. 11) located in a nearby social resource such as a library or school. This first descriptive response to questions about the neighbourhood then formed the foundation for responses to a new set of Problem Situations which invited people to transform their associated behaviours and values (Fig. 12). People externalised representations to an open question, to which there was no right or wrong way to respond, anything recorded being considered valid. So while there was complete diversity of response from participants to a particular question, what acted as a visible common parameter was the depiction of an identifiable object or sign from the neighbourhood. For example, the mantelpiece above the fireplace in the front living room was perceived to have an important function as a social focus and point of personal reassurance for residents in the Greenford Project Area of the West London Social Resource Project, but which particular objects were positioned on it varied from participant to participant. Again, as had been the case with the earlier work in Nottingham, there was a bandwidth within which articulation of expression could take place.

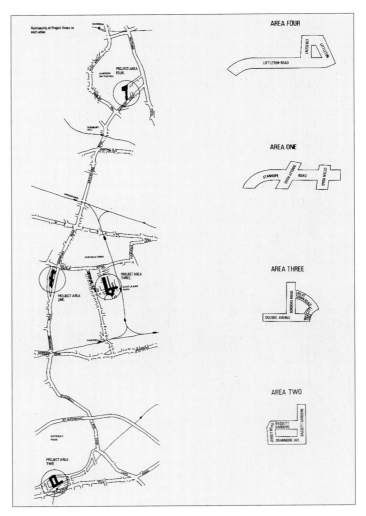

Fig. 9 *The West London Social Resource Project. Relationship of the four project areas to each other in outer west London.*

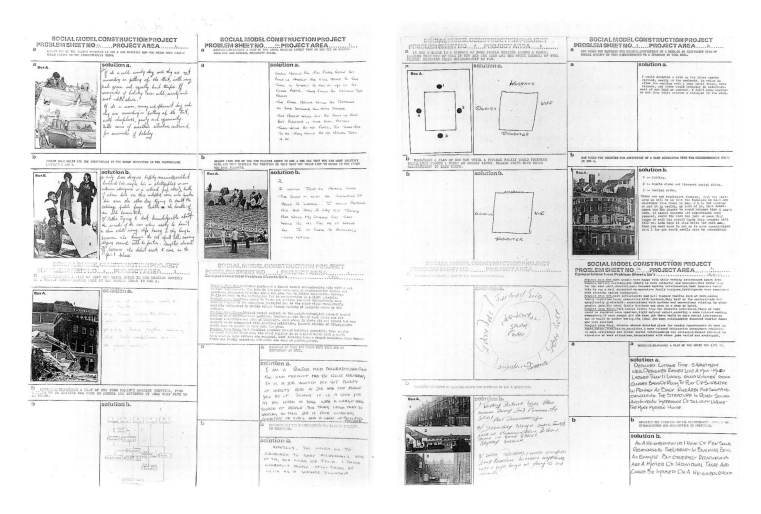

Fig. 10 *Completed response sheets. Examples from the Edinburgh Social Model Construction Project.*

13

A personal insight at this point was that there were definite patterns to the nature of signs, and to clusters of associated objects; they seemed to exist in groupings in which individual objects were seen as consistent with the overall grouping. I also became aware that the message from a display, such as the objects on the mantelpiece, was going in two opposite directions. First, there was the display to outsiders, passers-by, visitors to the house, constituting a kind of outface message: 'This is who I am, who I want to be, etc'. And then, in contrast, there was a more internal message directed at the building's occupants which provided them with a psychological context, a reinforcement for their own feelings of certainty and stability about who they were, their personal identity.

The above are purely personal observations, and in the actual responses received from participants there were no identifiable patterns of clusters and displays of objects and signs from which firm conclusions

Fig. 11 *West London Social Resource Project, Public Register Board, showing returns from the West London Manual.*

Fig. 12 *The West London Social Resource Project. Some completed pages from the West London Remodelling Book which invited participants to speculate on how they might change their environment.*

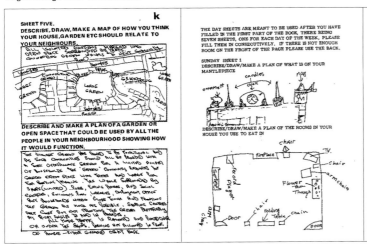

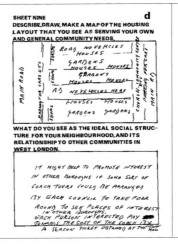

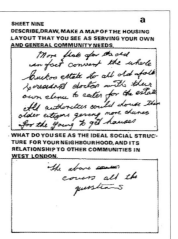

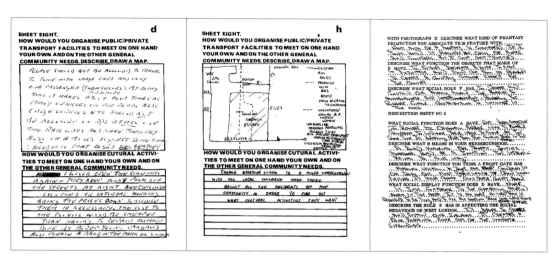

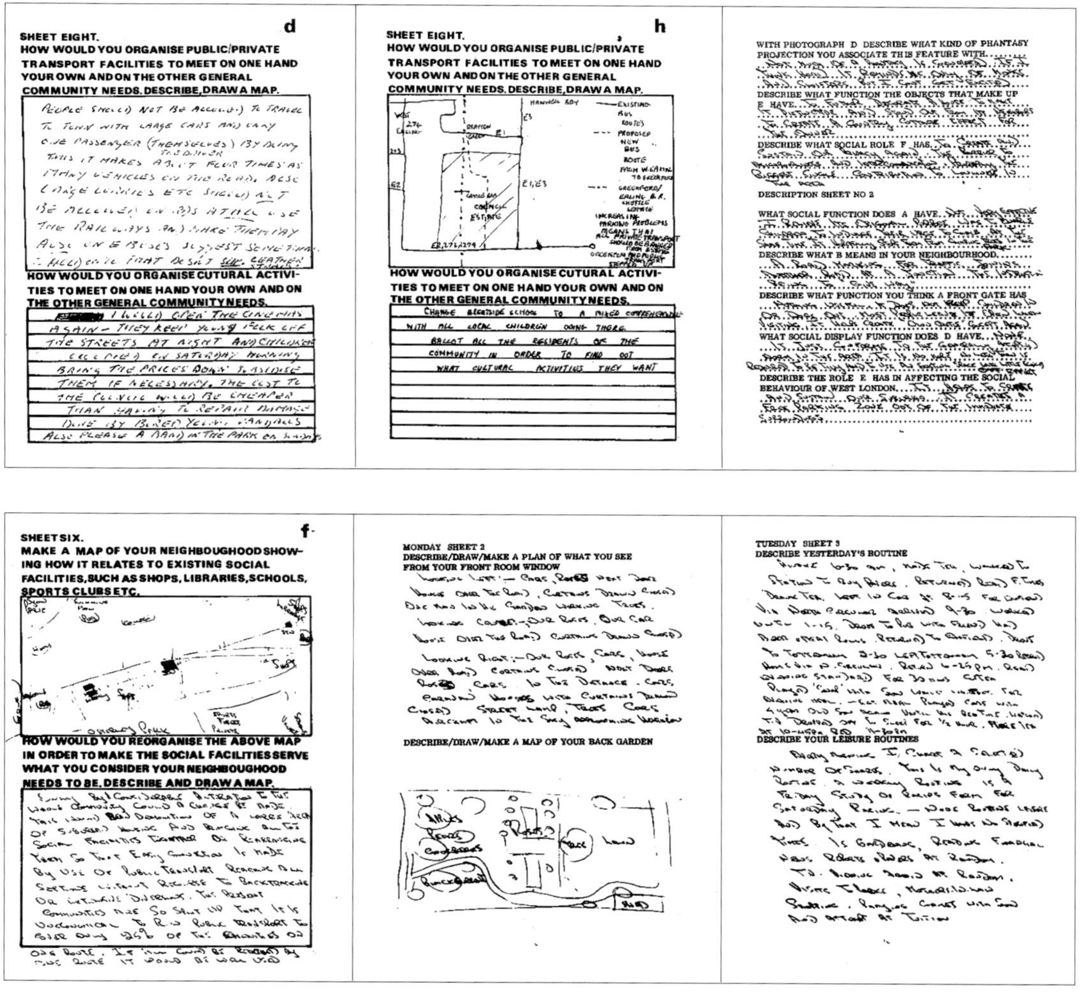

SHEET EIGHT.
HOW WOULD YOU ORGANISE PUBLIC/PRIVATE
TRANSPORT FACILITIES TO MEET ON ONE HAND
YOUR OWN AND ON THE OTHER GENERAL
COMMUNITY NEEDS. DESCRIBE, DRAW A MAP. **d**

[handwritten response]

HOW WOULD YOU ORGANISE CUTURAL ACTIVI-
TIES TO MEET ON ONE HAND YOUR OWN AND ON
THE OTHER GENERAL COMMUNITY NEEDS.

[handwritten response]

SHEET EIGHT.
HOW WOULD YOU ORGANISE PUBLIC/PRIVATE
TRANSPORT FACILITIES TO MEET ON ONE HAND
YOUR OWN AND ON THE OTHER GENERAL
COMMUNITY NEEDS. DESCRIBE, DRAW A MAP. **h**

[handwritten map]

HOW WOULD YOU ORGANISE CUTURAL ACTIVI-
TIES TO MEET ON ONE HAND YOUR OWN AND ON
THE OTHER GENERAL COMMUNITY NEEDS.

[handwritten response]

WITH PHOTOGRAPH D DESCRIBE WHAT KIND OF PHANTASY
PROJECTION YOU ASSOCIATE THIS FEATURE WITH.

[handwritten response]

DESCRIBE WHAT FUNCTION THE OBJECTS THAT MAKE UP
E HAVE.

[handwritten response]

DESCRIBE WHAT SOCIAL ROLE F HAS.

[handwritten response]

DESCRIPTION SHEET NO 2

WHAT SOCIAL FUNCTION DOES A HAVE.

[handwritten response]

DESCRIBE WHAT B MEANS IN YOUR NEIGHBOURHOOD.

[handwritten response]

DESCRIBE WHAT FUNCTION YOU THINK A FRONT GATE HAS.

[handwritten response]

WHAT SOCIAL DISPLAY FUNCTION DOES D HAVE.

[handwritten response]

DESCRIBE THE ROLE E HAS IN AFFECTING THE SOCIAL
BEHAVIOUR OF WEST LONDON.

[handwritten response]

SHEET SIX.
MAKE A MAP OF YOUR NEIGHBOUGHOOD SHOW-
ING HOW IT RELATES TO EXISTING SOCIAL
FACILITIES, SUCH AS SHOPS, LIBRARIES, SCHOOLS,
SPORTS CLUBS ETC. **f.**

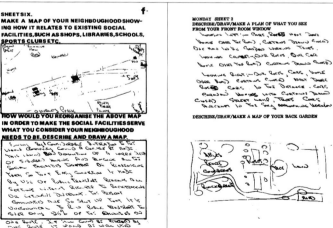

HOW WOULD YOU REORGANISE THE ABOVE MAP
IN ORDER TO MAKE THE SOCIAL FACILITIES SERVE
WHAT YOU CONSIDER YOUR NEIGHBOUGHOOD
NEEDS TO BE. DESCRIBE AND DRAW A MAP.

[handwritten response]

MONDAY SHEET 2
DESCRIBE/DRAW/MAKE A PLAN OF WHAT YOU SEE
FROM YOUR FRONT ROOM WINDOW

[handwritten response]

DESCRIBE/DRAW/MAKE A MAP OF YOUR BACK GARDEN

[handwritten map]

TUESDAY SHEET 3
DESCRIBE YESTERDAY'S ROUTINE

[handwritten response]

DESCRIBE YOUR LEISURE ROUTINES

[handwritten response]

Fig. 12 *Continued*

can be drawn that are transferable. The reason for this is simple. The Response Sheets on which problem situations were presented were purposefully phrased to be open ended, to elicit an expressive response to an open frame that externalised to the participant the very inherent relativity of perception and expression between individuals. However, clusters of objects can be seen to exist in identifiable locations, in places within the living room or on the facade of the building where their positioning is deemed permissible. Importantly, such permission is implicit and not explicitly articulated in a person's expression; it coexists within the plan. It was not until I started working with individuals who were outside the social environment of art in 1974, to develop a strategy in my work that would present their polemics from contemporary life directly within the gallery space of the art museum, that I was able to extend what I had noticed about personal transformation of space in people's responses to the West London Social Resource Project. A crucial part of my new strategy was to present the viewer of the work with a 'symbolic world', an encoded realm of photographic and text references, drawn from a particular context or environment associated with an identifiable polemic in contemporary life. The principal means of encoding the symbolic world (Fig. 13) was through a photographic documentation of a personal realm of references identified through the active involvement of an individual directly associated with it, and then by adding quotations and questions transcribed and composed from tape-recorded discussions with that same person. The participant was instrumental in giving the work its meaning for the viewer, for the participant entered into a process of loading the symbolic world with references that were clustered, and, more importantly, actual. For the symbolic world to function, it had to be believed by the viewer, the references consistent and belonging together.

The symbolic world was presented to the viewer in association with a question that would transform what was depicted into a problem situation for the viewer, who in response would perceptually link up discrete

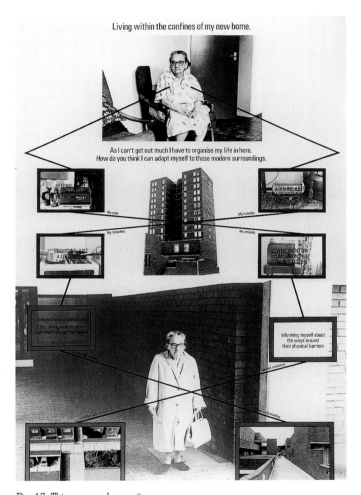

Fig. 13 *This page and opposite:*
'Living with Practical Realities', January 1978. Three panel work.
Each panel 76 cm wide x 109 cm high. Photographic prints,
Letraset text and mixed media. Collection Tate Gallery London.

Living with the present day limitations of a small income.

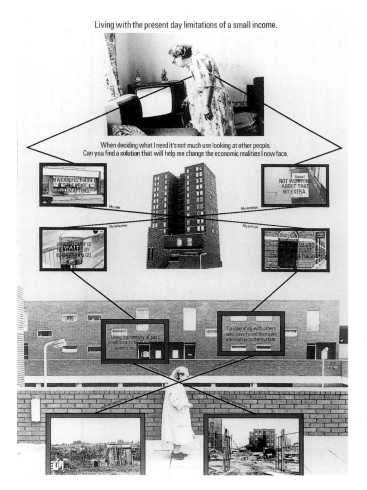

When deciding what I need it's not much use looking at other people.
Can you find a solution that will help me change the economic realities I now face.

Living without the certainty that I will see someone tomorrow.

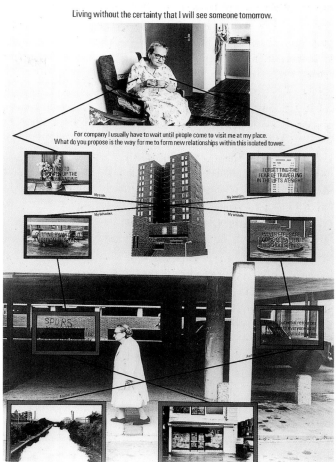

For company I usually have to wait until people come to visit me at my place.
What do you propose is the way for me to form new relationships within this isolated tower.

references, giving them their own perceptual bias. This encoding of references into a symbolic world was designed to give the viewer a realm of meaning in which a question could stimulate a relative response, or a solution that was open, there being no correct interpretation. Thus a sequence of different questions could generate a variety of ways of perceiving the same clustering of references in the symbolic world.

When pursuing my strategy of intervening inside the academic and rarefied world of the art institutions, the gallery, the museum, I purposefully sought out contexts that would represent issues and realities from present day society that would be rich in diverse realms of references. I felt that most people lived in suburban housing developments, big or small, and consequently I should look for a symbol of this environment, to locate the symbolic world and give it an extra meaning through its familiarity, thus also aiding its accessibility. This desire and subsequent search by car through endless suburban developments in West London led me to the idea of the tower block since it was, I felt, a highly visible polemical symbol of the moment; even if you didn't live in one yourself, you would know all about them. I embarked on a series of works over a twenty-five-year period that have actively involved residents, individually and collectively, in the creation of works to be presented not just in art institutions but also actually within the environment of the tower block itself.

As already stated, initially what interested me about the tower block was its message: its outface radiated an outlook for the future, for example, by using concrete as an indicator of Modernism. While the inherent problems of high-rise living are now well documented, in 1974 such buildings were still seen by many residents as desirable places in which to live. Certainly in France (Fig. 13) and later, in 1980, working with residents of the Märkisches Viertel and Gropius Stadt in Berlin, the kind of stigma that so destroyed the desire to live in these buildings had not yet taken root. In the main, residents still felt good about being given

Opposite Fig. 14
'Les Problèmes de la Nouvelle Réalité'. January–June 1977. Four panel work. This work contrasted the views of residents in public and private housing about their new environment on the outskirts of Paris.

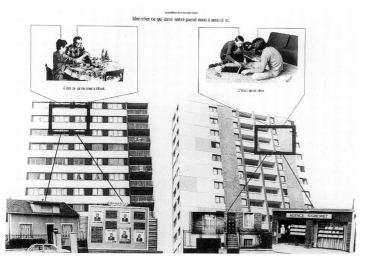

a flat in a tower block, even though there may have been serious uprooting from their personal past.

My first extensive association with residents of a tower block was at Skeffington Court, in Hayes, West London (Fig. 15) where I worked over a fifteen-month period during 1977/78 in the making of my project work 'Vertical Living'.[7] At this point residents were just beginning to question the environment into which they had recently moved and to which they were now adapting their lives. In the development of Skeffington Court the planners and architects had envisaged an environment which required a specified level of maintenance, both for its physical and its social infrastructure, the full time resident caretaker being an essential part of their plan. As financial cut backs took hold and the caretaker became part time, so what was a brand new building began to throw up increasing clouds of doubt for the residents, something I uncovered as my work developed. The work I was preparing, 'Vertical Living', looked at the existing environment in terms of Descriptive Models which became the basis for building Prescriptive Models; these would articulate and externalise how residents could envisage making changes to the environment of the tower and to their lives within and around it. So I set about defining with residents what they saw as problem situations that were to be articulated and encoded in a symbolic world and presented inside the tower block on 'Problem Displays'. There was a sequence of such Problem Displays, each made with a resident and which formed the main means of externalising the work's concerns to resident potential participants and other residents. In building up the participant group, my first contact with a resident was always at the front door, but subsequently I was asked in and these meetings were then held in the living room.

Although the building was an expression of uniformity in both its exterior and interior, this physicality providing a background message to everything that went on there, I soon began to register the diversity of expressions being made by residents inside their individual living space.

This page and opposite Fig. 15 *'Vertical Living'. Skeffington Court, Hayes, West London. 1978. Examples from a series of Problem Displays made with residents of Skeffington Court.*

VERTICAL LIVING

FIRST PROBLEM DISPLAY.

Looking at the effect on me of life in a confined space.

How can I reduce the amount of external noise that is disturbing my thoughts in here.

What do you think people like me can do to stop the feeling of isolation from others around them while being on their own.

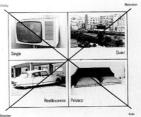

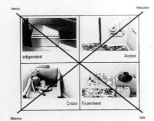

I began to notice that objects were placed in the living room in definite areas, that some objects were the focus of attention within the living room while others were on the periphery of vision. There were objects that implied the future, those that denoted actions, behaviours associated with the present, and those that created stability through connection with the past. Within the very rigid fabric of the building groupings of objects were confined to set locations, such as on the top of the television, side shelving, coffee table, etc. These articulations were in the main very much within the plan, as you might imagine the architect envisaging things. They were within the bandwidth of normality, what was permissible, and as all the residents were relativity new to Skeffington Court, perhaps this was to be expected. But I noticed that when someone had intervened in the space to change it, even in a small way, this change

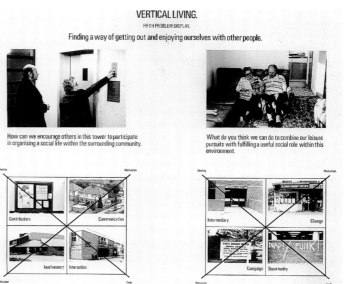

VERTICAL LIVING

THIRD PROBLEM DISPLAY.

Thinking about what we need to make home improvements.

How could viewing other people's ideas help create the impression of space within the confined area we were given.

What do you think we should do to arrange the interior of our flat around the way of life we want to lead.

VERTICAL LIVING.

FIFTH PROBLEM DISPLAY.

Finding a way of getting out and enjoying ourselves with other people.

How can we encourage others in this tower to participate in organising a social life within the surrounding community.

What do you think we can do to combine our leisure pursuits with fulfilling a useful social role within this environment.

had great significance for them, it was something special which they would point out. Within what at first sight might seem like a jumble of objects there was another category that could be from the past, present, future which psychologically extended the space inhabited by the person and connected them to the world outside. On the one hand residents arrange objects to exhibit their presence inside the space; on the other hand objects take them beyond the space. So both of these interventions by the resident had the effect of changing the fixed rigidity of the space for them, of combating the pressure to conform exerted by the space on their psychology.

This creation of psychological links between the inside and outside of the space was such a fundamental necessity for people that it became the central area of attention in a later work, 'Brentford Towers', 1986.[8] This was an evolving installation presented over a four-week period inside the tower block Harvey House (Figs. 16 and 17) situated in Brentford, West London, that was made with the active participation of the residents. A dominant factor of life within Harvey House were the large windows that were on two sides of the living room; while providing that important access to the world outside they also encoded it into a kind of living picture. The physical distancing of people from the external world, especially high up in Harvey House, was further reinforced by this 'picture window' encoding which gave a sense of unreality, of detachment. This unreality had the counter effect of enabling people to project themselves through the window pane on to the picture, releasing them from the confined remote reality inside the living room to form an imagined connection with some particular aspect of that picture.

When involved in the development of my work with residents I noticed that there, in the room, were objects that were important in facilitating this projection, and so I begun to ask people to create a descriptive channel between an object they possessed inside the living room with an object or some particular aspect of what they could see outside in the landscape beyond and then to imagine and describe a link.

Fig. 16 *Harvey House, Greendragon Road, Brentford, West London.*

Fig. 17 *'Brentford Towers', Harvey House, west London, 1987. One of a series of twenty-four display boards made with residents of Harvey House that were positioned on the landings throughout the building for a four-week period.*

Fig. 18 'The Lurky Place', as it was known locally, was an area of wasteland completely surrounded by various manifestations of contemporary urban society. It was situated at Hayes in outer West London.

All kinds of objects were selected, some obvious, some less so, but the selection was very imaginative. For example, household plants became a means of linkage with greenery outside; a keep fit bicycle was put into the living room so that the rider could imagine herself riding around a distant park; a lady looked for the same person everyday on a footpath, and felt she knew her, her budgerigar becoming the link in that projected relationship. The glass pane in the 'picture window' was an encoding plane that created the outside into a symbolic world, a world in which more free imaginative associations could be made than were possible purely from within the confined reality of the actual interior space. The window pane as an agent was the boundary between realities into which one had to pass, and this act enabled imaginative transformations, wanderings and projections. Often these projections gave the person a feeling of being in the company of other people, especially marked if they were living on their own. So people required a symbolic framework to release themselves from the background determinism of their living environment; the window was the boundary between psychological realities and an object was often the agent for creating a passage between them that enabled their interconnection.

The role of the boundary and its position in the journey between realities also played a big part in my project on the Avondale Estate, Hayes, West London, in the late 1970s and early 1980s. The work centred on the relationship of life on the estate with an adjacent wasteland known locally as 'The Lurky Place' (Fig. 18).[9] I had revisited the wasteland areas of West London, having come back from Berlin where I had been for some two years, developing four works that were presented in the exhibition '4 Inseln in Berlin'[10] at the Nationalgalerie, Berlin, in December 1980. The works in Berlin, which led directly on to the work in 'The Lurky Place', had all centred on various ways in which individuals had created their own expressive space, despite the pressures of being an island, a physical as well as an ideological island in which projections of Western free-market culture were heavily invested. An island within an island. You didn't need to visit Berlin at that time to know what it stood for as a beacon. Two practical experiences I had in Berlin led directly to the wasteland work in London, acting as a precedence for it, so are relevant to mention here.

While working with residents of a large housing block situated near the Berlin Wall in the Märkisches Viertel in North Berlin I came across drawings obviously made by children congregating at the bottom of buildings where they lived (Fig. 19). These drawings were so often a poignant critique of the surrounding modernist environment, a comment on daily life, that I became fascinated. They were quite outside the plan, and had the effect of changing the surrounding space, of making it more personal. When I talked to the children who had made the drawings I found that they were all created by different groups in the building in which they actually lived, and that they had not been drawn by a lone individual, but were the result of group activity; their creation was an agent for community. Later, when I had made an extensive documentation of the drawings, I contrasted the discussion I was having with the children with their parents' thoughts about the environment. It became apparent that the children, through their imaginative drawings, had created their own temporary escape from the confines of the rigid concrete determinism in which they were growing up, and that the act of going beyond what was permissible in the grown-up world was important to the drawings' meaning.

In complete contrast to the Berlin Wall drawings the other work, 'Organising My Means Of Escape' (see page 94), developed out of a collaboration between myself and an elderly lady living in the back house of a run-down traditional Berlin building at Kaiser-Friedrichstrasse, just off the fashionable Kurfurstendam. Frau Hannebauer had her own personal means of escape from her dark single room apartment, a route which led to her wonderful Schlabergarten at the Kolonie Ronnestrasse at Halensee. Once through the door in her garden she entered another realm of values that was quite hidden, even in opposition to the modern

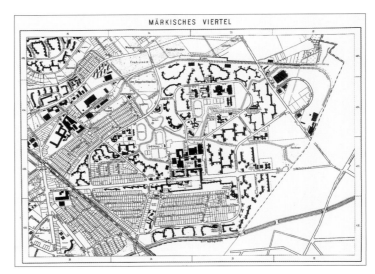

Fig. 19 *The Märkisches Viertel, North Berlin.*

Fig. 20 *Charville Lane Estate viewed from the surrounding wasteland*

world of the Kurfurstendam just outside her apartment. The Schlabergarten was born out of the idealism prevalent at the turn of the twentieth century which encouraged working people living in inner-city tenement blocks to have the possibility of contact with nature and community by renting a small plot of land, rather like an English allotment, but here to create a garden in which to relax and be oneself. Inside her own Schlabergarten Frau Hannebauer had actualised her own expression of 'nature' and retained links to her past inside the high wired fences that she had put up around her own garden. This contrast with the whole ethos of the 'Kolonie', which centred on the community and social values that were being maintained despite seemingly being torn apart in the free-market message of West Berlin at that time.

The children in the Märkisches Viertel found corners, odd spaces at the bottom of buildings as a context, an environmental space for their activities, and Frau Hannebauer likewise had needed a context, be it an officially enclosed one, in which to express personal perceptions and values. In both contexts there was a journey; in the flats at the Märkisches Viertel, the entry in the lift was the moment of transition between realities, and for Frau Hannebauer it was the closing of one door, the bus she caught outside her apartment every time she visited her garden, and the passing through the main door of the Kolonie. This idea of a symbolic journey between realities being an important unlocking procedure, a means of releasing oneself bit by bit, of recognising the distance between realities, and consequently the idea of a symbolic journey became an important feature of my work in 'The Lurky Place'.

On my return from Berlin to London in 1980, I initiated a search for a similar symbolic context to the ones I had found in Berlin, one in which an individual or group had self-organised and externalised their own creative expressions within a restricted and determined environment. I revisited many wasteland areas I had documented in the early 1970s, one of these being 'The Lurky Place' (Fig. 20). What was so special about 'The Lurky Place' was that though a large physical area, it was completely surrounded by a highly visible, dense and very active urban infrastructure. The wasteland was bounded on one side by a large gas works, on another by a canal and railway, by a concrete manufacturing plant, car and scrap metal yard, school, and then several large housing estates, so that there was a highly visible contrast in languages emanating from these various sites.

On previous visits to 'The Lurky Place' I had noted that when people went into the wasteland they did so to engage in pursuits that were not permissible in the surrounding society and that they nearly always took an object with them.[11] These objects were usually agents for a particular activity, an imagined pursuit or identity; they became the means of being someone else, and they were often discarded en route or after the event, in fact the wasteland was full of all sorts of debris transported there as part of people's associations with the place. Of particular symbolic significance to me was the large modern, grey concrete housing estate of tower and slab blocks that abutted directly on to one edge of the wasteland. The housing estate itself was contained, separated from the suburban semi-detached houses nearby, and was reached by a single long road from Hayes High Street. Daily life on the estate was to have been facilitated by the building of a parade of shops, community centre, etc in its middle, but though the place was only ten years old, these shops were by 1980 all now derelict and boarded up. From my initial walk over to 'The Lurky Place' from the estate centre, I had seen that the wasteland must have had an enormous pull and role as an available resource in people's lives there, especially for younger residents; the numerous holes in the dividing fence and worn footpaths leading away from the estate and into its interior bore testimony to this. On earlier visits to 'The Lurky Place' I had just documented objects I had found in the wasteland, now I wanted to work with a resident from the estate who regularly made a journey into its overgrown interior with its abandoned fields, woodland scrub and bushes.

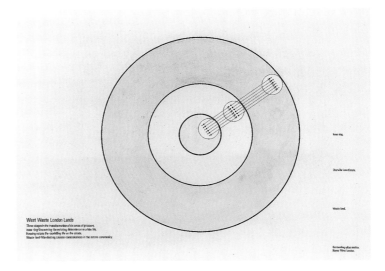

Fig. 21 *'West Waste London Lands. Three Stages in the Transformation of Six Areas of Pressure', 1981. 90 cm wide x 64 cm high. Ink, Letraset text, pencil on paper. Charville Lane Estate, West London.*

After meeting several residents of the estate, it became clear that while the wasteland was used by people of all ages, it was in the teenagers' lives that it played an extra role and had significance. This age group had not been represented very much in my art practice, so when I was introduced to Pat Purdy by her mother I felt ours was going to be an important collaboration. I worked with Pat Purdy over some fifteen months, making journeys from her personal room in the confined box that passed for a family flat, through the wire fence into the wide expanse of the wasteland. The destination of many of these journeys was the small improvised camps, often used for glue sniffing, that groups of teenagers had built using the cover of the wasteland to hide themselves from being seen by the world outside. Inside the estate itself, there were also all sorts of nooks and crannies in and around the buildings where groups of estate kids of all ages hung out for long periods of time, especially when it rained, claiming the space as their own (Fig. 21). At the point I came to work on the estate, most of the services associated with its upkeep had been withdrawn or were seriously depleted and so the various groups of younger children and teenagers were more or less left to themselves.

The inside of the slab blocks on the Avondale Estate were very isolating and depressing to anyone visiting, let alone living there, with their long corridors of uniform front doors, no natural light and grey concrete. So perhaps it was to be expected that contexts would be created in the buildings which could be personalised by various activities such as wall drawing, carving or making holes into the fabric of the walls, by scavenging old car tyres, discarded bits of furniture and placing them around the space. Although these actions were vilified by the authorities, my reaction was that this was fundamental creative behaviour, for it necessitated the psychological transformation of reality from institutional to personal space. The spaces for hanging out were thus contexts for creating community; to this end the intervention on the surface of the building was creative in the transformation of the space while also signalling the group's alienation from the governing values of institutional society, and reinforcing the interpersonal society between participants in the group. This fundamental act of transformation was largely psychological, for apart from symbolic gestures of making holes in the concrete facade, drawing on the walls, etc, they couldn't alter the environment physically, they could only change their approach to it, make a journey somewhere else, or get out altogether. Thus the journey into the wasteland, 'The Lurky Place', continued these acts of cognitive transformation, for once beyond the car park, the back of the garages and through that hole in the fence, a realm was entered into in which an anarchistic freedom was suddenly made possible. The camps were fashioned from things found lying around the estate that could readily be transported into 'The Lurky Place' and from items such as old car seats, galvanised metal sheeting, chicken wire and other discarded building materials. Through working with Pat Purdy I came to realise that in the process of transporting the items the wasteland they were actually invested with a new meaning, and became symbolic catalysts for the creation of the group's own society. The camps — temporary ephemeral structures — not only enclosed the group in a capsulised reality so that they felt free there, but also functioned to hide them from external scrutiny. In this latter respect camps were usually constructed in dense undergrowth, or occasionally were dug out underground. In 'The Lurky Place' I saw parallels with the situations I had worked with in Berlin, for both contexts were environmental and psychogical islands surrounded by another world of norms and values. An island within an island had been constructed.

This important representation of self-organisation as an island within an island was taken a step further in my work in the early 1980s by a chance meeting in a street in Earl's Court. This meeting led me to develop the symbolic reality of the wasteland into another sphere, in the representation of the small self-organised clubs that proliferated in London during the early 1980s. I had bumped into Kevin Witney, a painter, and he had told me about the Cha Cha Club he had just left, and

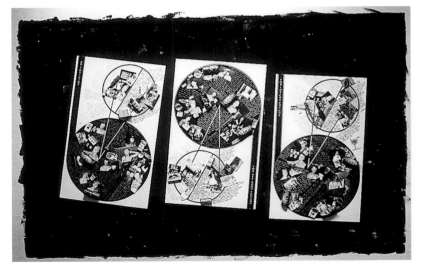

a whole new world was then graphically described by him which I immediately felt was excitingly relevant to the idea of 'creative transformation' and 'self-organisation' (Fig. 22). As a reaction against the idea of professionalism, and to the mass-market culture, groups of young people were starting to create and define their own contexts within which they could express their own sensibilities, externalise their own feelings of identity. While the development of these diverse subcultures, with their ethos of DIY and self-organisation, originated in the mid-1970s, aspects of what they were doing can be traced back to the 1950s, but by the early 1980s confident modes of expression of language had evolved that externalised beyond the confines of these islands, and visibly, aggressively outfaced with society.

I started an association with the Cha Cha, gradually getting to know most of the people associated with the club. It immediately became apparent that inside the small railway arch, painted black, and reached down a labyrinth of dark alleyways underneath Charing Cross Station in the centre of London, had many parallels with the camps in the wastelands, and with what I had found in Berlin. One immediate parallel was that a group of individuals had made a journey, from context to context, and facilitated their passage by an expressive personal language, through codes of dress that separated them from the world through which they passed. However, once those individuals had reached their island, in between, once through the entrance procedure at the door, for the duration and in that context they became a dynamic community. Of course, the network of relationships would exist once people were outside the club again, but then it would be extended, between the personal domains individuals had created for themselves, from within their living environments. In my work I was at first attracted to the self-organising club environments which individuals had created, these people acting as catalysts for the groups of which they were a part. They were the dynamic engine of the various subcultures that existed at that moment in the early 1980s. But as I got to know people I began to realise that their

Fig. 22 *Installation at the Arnolfini Gallery, Bristol. 'Are You Good Enough for the Cha Cha Cha?' 1982. Collection Tate Gallery, London.*

living environments were where the most significant statements of creative transformation were being made. Statements that connected directly to the ideas being pursued here. For during the 1980s, much council property, especially flats in those modernist estates, had become so stigmatised that they were even becoming empty and were very difficult to re-let and were even being boarded up and left derelict. And this while private accommodation seemed almost nonexistent and anyway far too expensive for the young and unemployed. So many of these empty flats on difficult run-down estates were taken over by young people, representing quite distinct subcultural groupings. They either squatted or the flats were let by the authorities to them just to get people back into them.

The economic ideology of the late 1980s and early 1990s led to a general withdrawal of services from what were often high density design, cheaply built large buildings on massive estates; the result was almost universally depressing, leading to a broken down, filthy and dangerous atmosphere. At this point many of the original inhabitants, perhaps like the people I had met in the early 1970s who had then been so optimistic about going to live on these estates, were now completely disillusioned, cynical and angry so that their one objective seemed to be to get out; and if they couldn't, and if there was no prospect of them going elsewhere, they felt trapped. So when the new Post Punk generation moved on to the estates, the message of poverty radiating from every nook and cranny of the environment and that of their own personal poverty made the transformations they created inside their flats even more significant. These transformations were often direct interventions into the environment of the estate in that they set up a visible capsule defined by a language that proclaimed its separation from their neighbours, ie the original inhabitants. There was no attempt to join the community, to become good estate residents, to live within the plan, and often attempts by other residents to set up community organisations to do something about the situation were just seen as a waste of time. The materials and objects used in the making of these transformed environments were often

Fig. 23 *'Taboo Housing Estate'. October 1982. 145 cm high x 92 cm wide. Photographic prints, Letraset text, ink, acrylic paint, pencil and found objects, collected by Scarlett. Owned by The British Council.*

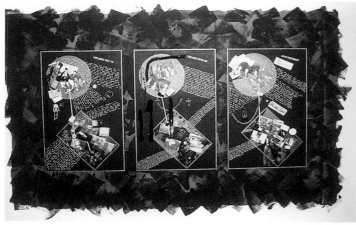

Above: Garry, Liz and Dave in their Acton flat.
Below: Fig 24 *Installation 'Escape With Us Into the Night', 1988.*
Each panel 140 cm x 90 cm. Three-panel work. Collection Rochdale Art Gallery.

tacky discarded items, debris found in the street or in building skips, which were then effectively recycled, and embodied into another language, given a new meaning that reinforced the psychological feeling of belonging to a subculture. These were positive interventions and transformation of space that gave the person who initiated them a strong feeling of personal identity, and of the future. For example Scarlett, who developed the work 'Taboo Housing Estate' (Fig. 23), had painted all her walls, floors and ceilings blood red, so that you were submerged, taken over by the domain of the island.

The composition of expression within these islands differed from the phenomenon of placing new, individual objects or special heirlooms in the living room in juxtaposition with other objects that I had noted, for these recycled, often discarded and found objects were 'imaginatively' put together to create a total environment, to make a statement. Not all these interventions and transformations took place in flats within modern housing blocks. Many that I visited were in generally run-down terraces, often located in the suburbs. One example of this setting occurred in the making of the work 'Escape With Us' (Fig. 24) where I met a group, Garry, Dave and Liz, who had taken over a floor of a semi-detached house in Acton, West London and painted it entirely matt black, placing inside the small rooms all kinds of marcabre icons associated with night and death, as an expression of what they called 'black culture'.

When I asked Garry, Dave and Liz what would happen to their way of life in the future, they replied, 'We will be like this forever', but within a month they had all moved out and on. The reality is that all these transformations to space were temporary affairs, often as ephemeral as the materials used in their making and it was this very transience that I felt gave these statements an added significance. For they demonstrated the basic importance of the creative transformation of physical and psychological space, in going beyond established norms for behaviour, for the future dynamic of culture, where nothing is fixed, nothing certain. This kind of fluidity is an important element in a society increasingly built on networks of exchange, where psychological realms can be moved and created in response to the desire for change. It is our psychology that gives order to the reality we build and create individually in a realm of collective pressure through society. The simple upshot of this individuality is that there can be many interpretations of the same encounter with reality. This implicit desire to express the self could not be more clearly demonstrated than when I visited those people in large blocks of flats, inhabiting identical planned spaces, where behaviour had been so carefully mapped out for the occupants. But their response, even in the selection and placing of ordinary objects in their living room, had been to create a denial of the given space and to replace it with their own realm of past, present and future. As previously discussed, this implantation in the space tends to be within a bandwidth of acceptable behaviour, being fixed for stable generations. Yet the often highly unstable occupancy of difficult-to-let flats by the Post Punk generation, generally younger and single, generated a more volatile tangential expression that went well beyond what had typically been envisaged by municipal architects and planners of the 1960s.

The inherent message of creative transformation, and self-organisation as a parameter for individual expression of the self, is an underlying concern in all my work with people in very different circumstances and environments, whether by adapting, altering or arranging existing languages, by working within bandwidths of what is acceptable, or making that journey beyond the topology of societal norms into the uncharted territories beyond. As I expressed in my work with individuals drawn to the cover of the night, it is in these hidden realms of expression that sensibilities that will shape future culture are born, and are then important to us all.

In the following collection of texts, and interviews with some of the people I have worked with over a twenty-year period, I hope to provide the reader with a few imaginative tools for thinking about the relationship of living space, its organisation, with the creative expression of people.

References

1. Among the sources which I found particularly influential were the following: *The Mechanisation of Thought Process*, National Physical Laboratory, Teddington. Vols 1 and 2. Collection of papers from the symposium held in 1958. Stafford Beer, *Decision and Control*. John Wiley: London, 1966. F H George, *Cybernetics and its Importance for Society*. Monograph 1, Institute of Cybernetics, Brunel University. Donald McKay, *Information Mechanism and Meaning*. MIT Press: Cambridge, Mass, 1972. Gordon Pask, *Physical and Linguistic Evolution of Self Organising Systems*. Systems Research: London, early 1960's.

2. For a more extensive discussion of issues concerning the social meaning and function of art practice in contemporary society, especially the role of the audience, please refer to three publications of mine: Willats, *The Artist as an Instigator of Changes in Social Cognition and Behaviour*. Gallery House Press: London, 1973. Willats, *Society through Art*. HCAK: The Hague, 1990. Willats, *Art and Social Function*, 1976. Reprinted Ellipsis: London, 1999.

3. Willats, *The Artist as an Instigator of Changes in Social Cognition and Behaviour*; Willats, *Art and Social Function*.

4. I refer the reader to the work of Basil Bernstein who defined two types of code, elaborated and restricted. Bernstein, 'Social Class and Linguistic Development: A Theory of Social Learning', in his *Education, Economy and Society*. New York, 1961, p 288

5. A complete description of the development and operation of the West London Social Resource Project is given in *Leonardo*, vol 7, pp 155–8; see also Willats 'Art and Social Function: Prescriptions', *Art and Artists*, June 1973, vol 8, no 3., and Willats *Art and Social Function*, Ellipsis: London, 1999.

6. 'Edinburgh Project' (discusses the social model construction project), *Art and Artists*, January 1974, vol 8, no 10. Willats, *Art and Social Function*.

7. Willats, 'The Counter Consciousness in Vertical Living', *Control Magazine*, November 1979, no 11, p 4

8. Willats, *Society through Art*. Also Willats, 'Brentford Towers', *Aspects*, Newcastle, winter 1985/86, no 31.

9. Willats, *The Lurky Place*. Published by the Lisson gallery, London, 1978. Willats, *The New Reality*. Published by the Orchard Gallery, Londonderry, Northern Ireland, 1982.

10. A discussion about this work and others made in Berlin in the late 1970s is reproduced in Willats, *Leben in vorgegebenen Grenzen–4 Inseln in Berlin*. Published by the Nationalgalerie, Berlin, 1981.

11. Another important area of wasteland used in my work was that at Charville Lane in Hayes, outer west London, where I made the works 'Two Worlds Apart' and 'The People of Charville Lane' (1981). The role of the wasteland surrounding the Charville Lane Estate, and the works I made with the residents of the estate are extensively discussed in Willats 'Two Worlds Apart' (Part 1), *Aspects*, Newcastle, no 16, autumn 1981, and 'Two Worlds Apart' (Part 2), *Aspects*, Newcastle, no 17, winter 1981/82.

12. Willats, *The New Reality*.

13. Willats, *Intervention and Audience*. Coracle Press: London, 1986. Willats, *Means of Escape*. Published by Rochdale Art Gallery, 1984.

The emergence of a new reality

The tower block at Skeffington Court, Hayes, West London. I saw this tower block as a powerful institutional symbol that exerted an all-embracing deterministic influence over residents' daily lives.

It is a significant factor in contemporary living that during the last fifty years our conceptions of, and expectations from, the everyday world have become more predetermined and at the same time more complex. A 'new reality' both social and physical has emerged that is authoritatively shaped and controlled by 'institutions' which have the function of manifesting the ideological foundations of our culture into people's daily lives. The 'new reality' is specifically a product of planning: planning how people should live in an urban society that is to be kept stable within the pre-fixed limits, norms and priorities of the higher authority that has been vested in institutions. There is, right from the start, an obvious basic division between the minority who determine the topology of urban living and the majority who are forced to passively accept its given form in their daily lives.[1] For decision-making, responsibility has been put in the hands of the professional, the specialist, the planner, the architect, the social worker and associated experts who impress their social consciousness into the actuality of other people's physical and social reality.

It is the reality in which people live and work that is the most important to them. So it is in these areas that our culture expresses overtly the ideological consciousness upon which it is founded, for they are the most likely source of social conflict, and thus these are the basic areas that need to be stable and controlled to ensure that its fabric remains unchallenged. What is recognised in the planning of the 'new reality' is that there is a very strong connection between the way in which a person forms their social consciousness and the physical environment in which they live and work. So increasingly the topology of the everyday world has come under the influence of the professional, the architect, the planner, the social worker and thus reflects their own norms, values and aspirations. Integral to the concept of the 'new reality' is that it is new, planned, a better way of living for large numbers of people. It is therefore important for the professionals in their conceptions to create a separation from the past or from ways of life that run counter to the norms and conventions of the dominant culture. The career pressures on the professional to create such a separation are considerable and have led to the 'newness' of the 'new reality' being constantly proclaimed; it has also led to a self-referenced uniformity and bleak repetitiveness in the physical form that it has been given.

Institutions

'Institutions' established by society to ensure that the physical environment and people's social behaviour remain under its determining influence manifest themselves in a wide variety of ways. These 'institutions' range from planning departments of municipal authorities to community centres, schools, newspapers, television, etc. In fact, one view of contemporary society is that it is comprised of a network of interlinked institutions, all of which agency various areas of control over society. Thus the explicit intention in establishing institutions is generally to preserve the status quo as determined by the decision-makers.[2]

The influence of these institutions on shaping the physical world of the 'new reality' lies within four broad areas:
1   maintaining and preserving the status quo;
2   enforcing norms and codes of behaviour;
3   providing a point of reference;
4   providing idealised symbols for people to emulate.
These institutions present themselves, and are legitimised, by the rest of society as bodies invested with expert knowledge; this authority is reinforced by the distance created between them and the people whom their decisions will effect.

The repetitive angular concrete of the 'new reality', embodied here in a walkway on the Lisson Green Estate, inner London.

The desk of the 'professional' is an authoritative symbol that creates a buffer, or separation from the world being determined. This desk belongs to an insurance broker working in the City of London.

The World of Objects

The ownership of property is a parameter to the fabric of Western society, its acquisition and maintenance underlying the structure of values from which the culture derives. The power given to property is symbolised through the possession of objects, especially those objects that can reinforce the idealisations projected through society's fabric of institutions. A constant pressure is exerted on the consciousness of the individual generated by specially constituted institutions, i.e. advertising agencies, broadcasting corporations, newspaper empires, etc., to view the world as a world comprised of objects.[3] More specifically a world of those objects that have been created and approved, because of the deterministic influences that are associated with their acquisition and their use. This pressure exerted through media constraints, such as women's magazines, television, billboards, is so great that not only are other people perceived as objects, but the self also. In this position the individual is passive, and moulded by external forces, for in order to possess objects, or to emulate the possibility of their possession, behaviours and attitudes associated with those objects have to be conformed with.

The desiring of objects has the effect of orientating people away from involving themselves in any meaningful relationship with the community. Dominating modern life is a two-way neutralising pull on the consciousness of the individual: one the basic drive to conform to group norms, the norms implicitly held by any really functioning community; the other to subsume the values of human involvement beneath that of involvement with the desire to possess objects. The latter pull is enormously strong, for the associative behaviours and attitudes given to the possession of objects psychologically provides and replaces the norms and values that are deficient because of a lack of community involvement. There is an important difference between the two ways through which social attitudes and values are assimilated by the individual; in that those acquired from direct involvement with the community will be more overtly in accordance with the community's circumstances and its needs. These community attitudes and values may well be in conflict with the surrounding institutional structure within which that community has to exist, while those the individual acquires through attending to the possession of objects are more easily predetermined by the institutions that generated those objects in the first place. It is thus an important priority of those institutions that people perceive themselves as wanting to live within a world comprised of objects, the objects of implied power.

Separation from Nature

The exercise of control over the so-called 'natural environment' in order to survive is a fundamental task of any society. In the 'new reality' this control is continually impressed on the consciousness of people through encoding the physical environment into a highly complex structure of interrelated symbols that exhibit their separation from nature. This control is greatly emphasised by stating a high degree of technological achievement in the formation of rigid structures into blocks and towers, and then by creating a highly defined boundary around them. These developments are not just removed from nature but are separated by their defined boundaries from other urban developments near by. Thus a housing estate, office block complex, shopping precinct, all exist in the professionals' conceptions as contained islands, and this is given an added symbolic meaning by delineating a boundary between the internal state's order and the disorders of nature externally. Nature is the symbol of the 'counter forces' of entropy, untamed and always moving towards anarchy, and is thus a threat to the stability of the infrastructure of society; it is therefore repressed.

While nature is repressed, certain natural elements are included in the plans of the 'new reality', but only as a demonstration of how they can be held within a fixed framework, again impressing on to the psychology of the inhabitants the degree to which they are living within

A view of the world below and its containment of nature from the top storey of an inner London residential tower block.

The separation and control of nature is emphasised in the new reality by isolating and encoding it within concrete.

a predetermined environment. Through the professional, society appropriates 'nature' and encodes it into its own system of beliefs and values, neutralising what is considered its disruptive potential and displaying instead isolated elements that are held up as its own cultural products.

Of special symbolic significance are the wasteland boundaries between the encoded order of the 'new reality' and the anarchistic wilderness of surrounding nature. Such wasteland boundaries not only exist between urban developments, but within them, where they take on a special meaning as discarded remnants that again constantly remind the 'new reality's' inhabitants of their own separation from nature.

The encoding process into symbols of order is achieved through a combination of media and form, such as in the use of concrete, aluminium, glass, etc. in the reduction of a building into angular, square, repetitive, monumental shapes. All this is constantly impressing on the consciousness of individuals that someone else is exercising control on their behalf over the natural elements that could disrupt the determined order in the world in which they live.

Living Space as Institution

The domestic interior 'living space' has become an important agent for our culture to symbolise its idealisations. It is the primary context for the ideological foundations of the dominant culture to be constantly stated to the individual and thus, ultimately, to the community. The 'living space' is encoded into an ideal type that is then projected, through the media, to the individual. By shaping the domestic 'living space' in accordance with the projected ideal types, an ideology is implicitly ever present and, like everything else in the 'new reality', what goes on can be under the constant shadow of society's institutions. The basic constructs in our consciousness of ourselves and others are moulded by that part of the environment in which we want to be most free and expressive. The physicality and inflexibility of the domestic living space's structural mass means that it is the inhabitants who must adapt as soon as they move in. This feeling of restriction and passivity is strengthened by the rules and regulations that accompany life within its confines. For the housing blocks' interiors do not adapt themselves to the inhabitants' requirements; the inhabitants cannot influence the planner of their own living spaces, they can only modify its surfaces and position objects within it to state their own identities and values.

While the layout and position of the housing block have been predetermined, so in a different, more subtle way, has the content. For the media also projects 'models' of preferred ways of life that are there simply to be emulated. The media's representations of the 'model' bring together various objects that denote forms of success, power, ability, etc., and these are stated to people as desirable attributes, the ones they should have themselves.[4] The inference being that a person will acquire these attributes by making similar arrangements with objects in their own homes.

Change in Social Climate

The optimism of the 'professional' initially in their planning of the 'new reality' has been replaced by the tension and fears of the people who actually have to live there [i.e. in housing blocks] today (1982). The 'new reality' as a controlled and considered entity was very much a product of our recent past (the 1960s), a period of growth and expansion, not just economically but socially; this was the period of liberalism in the infrastructure of society. Consequently the 'new reality' had embodied in its physicality elements that were seen as symbols for liberalisation, the potential of freedom in the set determinism of social relationships. Areas have been set aside between the blocks as focal points for interaction, areas of leisure, but always within a framework kept well inside a controlled overall plan. The spaces between the blocks were originally littered with small clusters of seats, benches set within concrete rectangles, all symbols of the liberal gesture within what was to be a well

The local shops provided for residents of the Avondale Estate, West London. Only one shop was operating (in 1982), the rest having closed because of vandalism.

Officially provided notice board on the Avondale Estate, West London. The ineffectuality of such official devices means that they are completely disregarded.

The car park under the tower block, Skeffington Court at Hayes, West London. The car park was considered so dangerous that residents were inhibited from using it for anything.

ordered, self-responsible community that would work in accordance with the laid down rules and their boundaries. Also, at the time of moving in, many residents viewed their new surroundings optimistically, its physicality symbolising a new way of living, 'the way of life for the future', this giving initially even feelings of euphoria at having arrived somewhere that the world was soon going to look like.

Initial optimism and just plain relief at having somewhere to live soon began to break down as the full implications of what residents were living in began to eat into the psychology of the individual. This, coupled with today's definite shift back towards a much less liberal social climate, with less wealth to acquire those objects that symbolise power and social status, and which double up for community involvement, has added a further dimension to inner tension, as there is nothing new with which to replace the resulting vacuum. Another very important factor in this breakdown is that the physical fabric of the 'new reality' was conceived as requiring a high degree of maintenance, and was made totally dependent on the active involvement of outside institutions for its support. The physical fabric of the 'new reality' and its institutional support structure were products of a time when it was possible for the professional to dream of an ideal environment, and of its inhabitants as dependants, and consider this as the natural state of affairs.

For this environment to function at all it actually requires people to conform to a high level of what is seen by the governing institutions as reasonable behaviour, and in conjunction with this it also demands the availability of economic and manpower resources to keep it all together and operating. When this support structure starts to be withdrawn, as is happening in the current climate (the climate of the early 1980s), the physical fabric starts to decay very rapidly and residents become increasingly distressed. Natural community patterns have been broken up by the rigid segmented physicality of the 'new reality', as have the old traditions of community self-reliance. The withdrawal and resulting break up of the support structure and the reduction of available services have accelerated the process of isolating the individual. People have been left adrift, psychologically abandoned and confused; they know the world around them is breaking down but they do not have the means, or now the motivation, to be able to respond. Feelings of optimism have been replaced by a repressed tension, and that tension is everyday life today for the inhabitants of the 'new reality'.

Repression of Expression
Virtually all means of expression for residents of the 'new reality' is denied except for what can be accomplished inside the crammed interiors of their own flats. All access to any means of communication is held by an authoritative institutional fabric that is there to govern everyday life, and which is perceived by residents, and purposefully so, as remote and removed. Any spontaneous resistance to pressures emitting from the 'new reality', such as the writing of graffiti slogans on the concrete walls, or through the development of forms of music such as Punk music, is finally, and often very quickly, eradicated either through a direct enforcement of institutional rules or through a more subtle subversion.[5] The grey walls of the blocks, their unyielding concrete and gravel surfaces, their repetitive box-like structures, the code of conduct laid down in the tenancy agreements are all elements that inhibit the externalisation of any attitudes and feelings.

In a similar manner to the means of production being owned by the dominant culture, so the means of communication and its articulation are the sole preserve, within the institutional fabric, of the 'professional'. Culturally legitimised and idealised forms of expression require technical resources and expertise far beyond the means and capabilities of ordinary people. People's attempts to express themselves, or to create interpersonal networks that are within their capabilities, are directly inhibited for they are shown to be amateurish, a status that confers a derogatory image. To be professional is seen as the only acceptable and desirable state for self-expression to have any validity, even in their own

Different forms of domestic dwellings stand for quite different social values. Private estate, Ruislip, West London.

Council estate, Hayes, West London.

Seat on the Ocean Estate, East London.

eyes. However, achieving professionalism is associated with considerable difficulty; special skills, knowledge and resources are all remote and out of reach of these people, and thus they become elements that inhibit even the motivation to try and publicly externalise resistance to the 'new reality's' pressures.

Hidden Tensions, Frustrations and Anger

Despite the hard, grey, cold exterior of the 'new reality's' concrete blocks, human emotions still exist, though as a hidden element that is revealed to the outside world only through the drawings and slogans on the walls of buildings, in the corridors and generally through evidence of vandalism to its physicality. Small informal networks of relationships, between neighbours, parents or within family groups generate reactions to the environment, but in the absence of any means of public expression they are bottled up, compressed into small knots that gnaw away at the inner self. Tension is fuelled by stories generated via neighbours, casual acquaintances met in the lifts and elsewhere, of muggings, break-ins, police activity, sex parties and so on. This has produced an uneasiness in people's outlook, reinforced, not surprisingly, with there being no jobs, little money and the sense of being trapped forever in a concrete block. In the end this gets to people to such an extent that it creates a sense of their own uselessness and ineffectuality. Consequently people are turning on what is nearest to them; ever-present and a reminder of their own miserable state, the concrete blocks themselves are coming under attack; the block they are living in, their own domestic world. They quite simply just want to smash it up and get out. However, there being no possibility of social mobility, or any economic mobility, and with no means of articulating their own feelings in the open, a general emotional state, initially of repression and then anger, builds up within the grey concrete walls of the blocks, emotion that is ready to break out into violent disorder.

The State of No Culture

An important, recent though negative development in the daily lives of people living within the housing projects of the 'new reality' has been the demise of their ability to generate their own culture. Traditional working class communities have long been associated with the making of their own special culture, which has been completely displaced in their occupancy of the 'new reality'. While it is not always the case, but generally so, people coming into a new housing project are rarely drawn from one community, their arrival relating to their individual circumstances rather than to those of a whole community. However, in time a new community might well be expected to form that would combat the initial displacement of residents and this would eventually generate its own forms of culture. The rapid turnover of residents, their drive to get out as fast as they can, and the segmented physical environment itself, completely militate against this happening.

Among young people, the section of the community with the most energy, spontaneous outbursts of creativity do break out and break through the surrounding restrictive environment. The strongest form that this energy takes is in music, usually initially created by messing about in parents' living rooms. Punk culture is the articulated response to the 'new reality', its motivation and form stemming directly from the repressiveness of the younger residents' environment. Punk music and clothes were an overt expression to the world outside of teenage alienation and their determination to fight back, though other equally important manifestations have been the 'fanzines' and different forms of dancing, such as the 'pogo'. The importance of Punk culture was in its contextualisation, for initially it came directly from the context to which it addressed itself; equally importantly, it was an aggressive confrontation with the notion of professionalism. You too could be a 'mini star', your individual self on your own housing estate; also the whole basis of DIY in Punk culture was a manifestation of self-organisation. However, Punk culture has gone the way of all forms of resistance to the institutional

The physical fabric of the Avondale Estate quickly started to deteriorate leaving a third of the flats uninhabitable after as little as fifteen years.

Graffiti on the Avondale Estate, West London. The grey concrete walls of the estate are covered all over with graphic traces of people's resistance to their surroundings.

Vandalism or creative expression? Avondale Estate, West London.

Residents of the tower block, Skeffington Court, West London, put plant pots outside their front doors to combat the uniformity of their physical surroundings, and also as a means of initiating contact with their neighbours.

fabric and been subverted by it, through being institutionalised itself, and thus it has given way to a state of no culture, for nothing has regenerated itself. Teenagers are now again being presented with idealisations to worship, a diversion from the crumbling fabric of the 'new reality' immediately around them. The state of no culture is the state of culture.

The Creation of a Parallel World

Important to people who are living within the 'new reality' and dominant in their daily behaviour is their fundamental fight back against the surrounding determinism. People simply don't want to give in easily and, despite the enormous pressures, there is a continual struggle to establish their own individual identity and retain contact with other people living where they live.[6] 'Counter consciousness' here exists as a kind of underground network within the 'new reality' and is a parallel world in enforced coexistence with its surroundings. Even without any formal organisation such as a tenants' association, residents find ways of trying to forge their own network of relationships with other residents, even if it is just with their immediate neighbours. The odds must be counted as definitely against people, but even so another world can be built (even if just symbolically) that shows that there is still the will to establish a different social consciousness of community based values.

There are still points of contact within the boundaries of the 'new reality', such as on landings and inside the lifts, and these become important contexts for establishing a 'counter consciousness'. For it only requires one or two articulate people to form a coherent picture of the environment, and have the motivation to react, to come into contact, for there to be the potential to establish organised meaningful communication. However, the totality of the isolating pressures in the 'new reality' and the interlinking between media and physical reality make the construction of a coherent total view extremely difficult. Generally, people's perceptual models of the surroundings in which they live are highly fragmented and contextualised, built on their own

43

immediate experience.[7] Such fragmentary impressions, reactions and tensions contribute significantly to people's inability to act for themselves. However, there is the chance for people to extend the boundaries of their contained lives by creating new territories of activity that can then become an active context for the creation of a parallel world. It seems that the alienation of the territory is very important for the manifestation of activities that are themselves alienated from the dominant culture, the culture from which people are trying to escape. The feeling of alienation is crucial and the key building block to the formation of an identity for those persons who go into the new territory. Here the mutual hatred of the 'new reality' is the catalyst for the formation of a larger community feeling that can be transferred back into everyday life within the confines of the housing estate.

Reactions to Pressure

Reactions by residents against the constant pressures of the 'new reality' are largely set up in response to a totality that is perceived as all-embracing, cold and authoritative, it makes all the rules and at the same time is removed and amorphous. 'Who do we deal with? The world seems full of faceless professional bureaucrats.' In their reaction, people's responses seem to fall into a number of categories, all of which can be associated in some way with the notion of 'counter consciousness'. Perhaps the most overt response is when people seek to destroy the environment in which they are trapped, either by directly vandalising it, or (depending on your viewpoint) by breaking it up by mis-using or re-using the facilities provided. Smashing windows, urinating in lifts, and general destruction of the environment are obvious expressions of residents' anger at being trapped there. About nine months after moving into their flat, a tolerance level is reached and a resident begins to realise their own isolation and become aware of the pressures around them. This is when the initial euphoria at the flat's newness has worn off; after that, tensions gradually build up to a point

Residents of the Charville Lane Estate, West London, banded together of their own accord to combat their isolation and social deprivation. Two devices residents established were the mini market, held at the estate centre once a month, where they recycled household objects, and the community disco.

Two of the many camps built in the wasteland adjacent to the Avondale Estate, West London.

when people just want to take apart what they can immediately see is causing their anguish.

At another, more subtle level, the destruction of the environment is not destruction at all, but is creative; people are simply registering their mark, showing that they exist. Acts of so-called vandalism as 'counter consciousness' are no more than anarchistic exhibitions of people's energies and individualism. Also acts of destruction are symbolic agents in establishing a 'counter consciousness'. For the group activities from which they arise, such as hanging around on stairways, destroying playground facilities, are rarely the activity of a lone individual, but are the work of a small group or gang.

On the other hand, formal organisations that register people's reactions to the pressures of the 'new reality', such as tenants' associations, while they might be the most obvious articulate response, are not necessarily the most effective. In fact, while a tenants' association must generate some cohesion by its very existence, and is an important agent in combating passivity, it is still not capable of fundamentally changing the physicality of people's situation. The important effect of such an organisation is social, and internal, between actively contributing residents, though for those not directly participating it can have the effect of putting the lid on a situation by seeming to cover up a potential opening for their expression.

Contexts for Manifesting Counter Consciousness

The unofficial nature of the contexts established to express 'counter consciousness' is essential to their power as agents, but of equal importance is their close relationship to the normal daily behaviours of residents. While wastelands adjacent or within the 'new reality' are a powerful context simply with which to identify, it is how they are used as agencies for specific activities, as diverse as track bike riding or glue sniffing, that is really significant. Other locations are used to hide in furtively, those parts of the 'new reality' that are the most screened:

stairways, lift landings, the complex of sheds provided for residents' storage; also garages, especially those that have been abandoned, the ones which always seem to have everyone's rubbish thrown in them.

Contexts for Counter Consciousness: the Transportation of Objects

Objects are important agents in the expression of 'counter consciousness'. However, in nearly all instances, their role is changed from the one assigned to them by the dominant authoritative culture from which they originate.[8] The dominant culture's ownership of the means of production requires that an object's use is either transformed from the one intended, or is extended into a territory in which 'counter consciousness' can be manifested. Here the object becomes an agent, as it is the means through which relationships are initiated and enabled within the group, or of facilitating fantasy roles constructed by the individual; for example, the walker in the wasteland with his air rifle and dog sees himself as the lone hunter in the forest, or some backwoodsman figure.

Instead of an object symbolically replacing relationships with other people, as in the dominant cultural consciousness, it becomes the means through which the pressures of that consciousness can be resisted. Objects are more tool-like, they are the trigger for exchanges between people and, by implication, their references extend into the community, and if they do not already have this characteristic as inherent, they acquire it through their transformation.

One particularly interesting transformation is exemplified by the can of glue, usually Evostick. In one context the can of Evostick has a deterministic, constructional role, i.e. in the making and repairing of objects. This is its positivistic role within the dominant culture. But this function is completely negated and transformed by young people sniffing the glue in order to get high. Even more significant is the transportation of the glue can into a wasteland where it is the prime agent for the building of a camp, an important context for generating group cohesiveness. The crucial factor is that the very alienation from the

Cars are driven by glue sniffers into the wasteland adjacent to the Avondale Estate and then set on fire.

dominant cultural norms of glue sniffing as an activity among young people is crucial to its function as their means of escape. Ultimately the most important form of glue sniffing is communal; the can of glue is burnt on a fire that forms the focal point of the camp, then, as part of the resulting anarchistic group high, other objects are transformed. Cars are driven into the wasteland and set on fire, then just left as rusting monuments to the group's activities, eventually to be taken over by the forces of the wilderness, and to find a harmony with them. This again is a specific transportation of an object from one context to the other. Small objects that are already lying around, or have been brought over to the camp by the group, are simply picked up and utilised, often with extreme points of energy. The 'can of glue' is a highly symbolic object in this context because of what results from its transformation as this in turn also results in other objects being transformed to act as agents for 'counter consciousness'. There are many other alien activities that involve transformation. For example, one extreme activity on the Avondale Estate, in Hayes, West London, involved tenants standing on the bath in their flat in order to put their ear against the air vent outlet, and from this everyone's conversations in the whole block could be heard, i.e. transformation air vent outlet to receiver.

Note: This chapter is comprised of extracts adapted from Stephen Willats, 'The New Reality', The Orchard Gallery, Londonderry, 1982. First published as part of the catalogue *The New Reality*, The Orchard Gallery, Londonderry.

References

1. These ideas are extensively explored in my essay published in Willats' *Living Within Contained Conditions*, MOMA: Oxford, 1978, and then later on in my exhibition catalogue, *Leben in vorgegbenen Grenzen – 4 Inseln in Berlin*, Nationalgalerie Berlin, 1980/81. Also refer to the extensive series of essays presented in *Marxism and the Metropolis*, for a very pertinent exposition of contemporary urban issues as they affect the 'new reality' of American cities. William K. Tabb and Larry Sawers, eds, Marxism and the Metropolis, Oxford University Press, 1978.
2. Stafford Beers, *Decision and Control*. John Wiley: London, 1966. This book presents an interesting critique of existing decision-making mechanism in society.
3. The relationship between different social consciousness and the perception of people and self as objects is presented in a paper by Dale Lake which I found particularly pertinent to my own thinking. The paper is titled 'Perceiving and Behaving', and is published by Teachers College Press, New York 1970. Also influential to my thinking were the studies presented in Charles Kiesler, ed, *Topics of Social Psychology*. Addison-Wesley: London. Particularly important to me were 'Conformity' by Kiesler and Kiesler 1970, and 'Group Performance' by Jones Davis, 1969.
4. Varda Langholz Leymore, *Hidden Myth: Structure and Symbolism in Advertising*. Heinemann: London, 1975.
5. While I was working in the Märkisches Viertel, North Berlin, a huge housing complex that epitomises my concept of the 'new reality', I noticed on the walls of the blocks and towers, drawings made by children. These drawings were not simple graffiti made in anger but drawings of an environment that was quite different from the ones in which the children were living. I started to photographically document the drawings and later I made some tape recordings of discussions with the children who had drawn them and with their parents. This material formed the basis for my book, *Ich lebe in einem Betonklotz* (Märkisches Viertel Berlin). This contrasts the 'new reality' of the grown up world of the adults with the fantasy world of the children. Willats, *Ich lebe in einem Betonklotz*. Buchhandlung Walther König: Cologne, 1980.
6. I think a very interesting and fascinating booklet was published by the tenants of the Honor Oak Estate describing how they perceived their history and current everyday life there. The booklet represents the tenants' own fight back against the anonymity of their surroundings. *A Street Door of Our Own*, Honor Oak Neighbourhood Association, 1–3 Forman House, Frensbury Road, London SE4.
7. Basil Bernstein has based his considerably influential theories on the contextualisation of language and thought patterns, what he calls 'Restricted Codes' and 'Restricted Thought Process'. A really good critique of Bernstein's theories is made by Harold Rosen, and his discussion is also relevant to the general assumptions made by the 'professional' about the residents of municipal housing schemes; see Harold Rosen, *Language and Class*. Falling Wall Press: Bristol, 1972.
8. 'The Lurky Place' is the name given to the large area of wasteland adjacent to the Avondale Estate, Hayes. Though I first came across 'The Lurky Place' in 1972, I did not start fully exploring it until 1976, and while doing so I was struck by the many functions this piece of discarded land had for the estate residents. I started to photographically document objects brought over to 'The Lurky Place' by residents to agency their activities there and which were then discarded. And from this documentation I produced my only landscape work to date, the book, *The Lurky Place*, published by The Lisson Gallery, London, 1978.

'Can Two Views Ever Really Co-exist?' Two panel work.
October/December 1983. Each panel 140 cm high x 101 cm wide.
Photographic prints, photographic dye, ink, Letraset text, acrylic paint and objects.

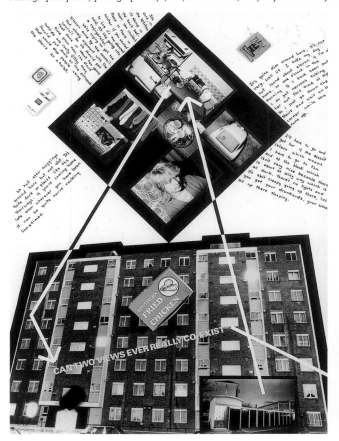
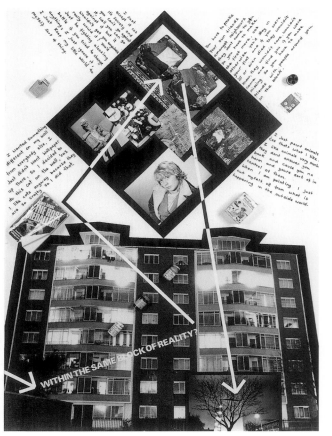

Personal space

Display board from ' Multistorey Mosaic' West London, 1990.

The very centre of an individual's self-organisation of personal space is usually the living room, and this takes on a special symbolic significance when this is a highly contained, ordered environment that is non-individual, then there is a psychological pressure on the occupant to assert their identity or just go under. The investment of the self into a space is often subconsciously undertaken rather than consciously articulated, the resulting display of a symbolic language being, it seems, inherent in social behaviour.

While most of the organisation and displays of objects, etc. are within the bandwidth of culturally approved norms and conventions, it is those personal, particular, and often small interventions to transform the immediate personal space that my engagement with people focused on in a series of art works created over the last three decades. I saw that these acts of transformation — sometimes little adaptations or subversions of the institutional specifications given for that space — were basic manifestations of creativity, resulting in something akin to personal empowerment. I saw that they were, therefore, acts of symbolic importance in approaching the world in which we all are now, and that they were encoded into the symbolic worlds I was presenting in my works as a model to which the audience could relate, as a heuristic tool for their own creative potential.

Another equally important act by residents of small, confined and isolated personal living spaces is to extend the psychological realm of that inner space into the fabric of the surrounding environment, an environment they can see but not touch. This linkage between the interior space to an aspect of the distant outside also created transformations in

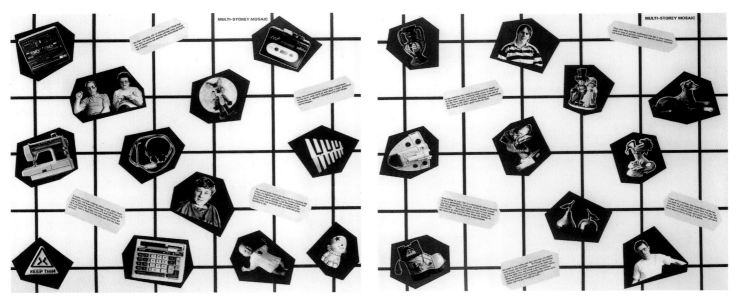

'Multi-storey Mosaic'. Feltham, West London. 1990. Made as a collaboration between two residents of the Highfields Estate.

an imagined sphere, and expressed the relativity inherent in our perceptions, in that we often see what we can create. Consequently, this aspect of people's personal space also became a focus of attention in my work.

This grouping of interviews under 'Personal Space' was made with residents of confined living spaces, and were all undertaken in association with the development of a work between me and them, as a collaboration.

Above: Highfields Estate, Feltham.
Right: Samuda Estate, Isle of Dogs.

Helen Treadway

Hunter House, Highfields Estate, Feltham,West London.
'Multi-storey Mosaic' Homecourt, Highfields Estate.
June 1980.

SW: So, looking around the room there are all these very particular kinds of objects around, some of which I have taken various photographs of. What kind of objects do you think are perhaps the most personally expressive, that you feel say something about you?

HT: The figurines and things I like collecting myself, and things I like to look at, have around me. I suppose they must say something about me, exactly what I am not sure, but I do like nice objects to look at and they're more traditional figurines rather than modern.

SW: So you like traditional things.

HT: I am more traditional, old-fashioned possibly if anything in my outlooks maybe as well as what I like. Other things that I have collected, the parrot was something we bought on holiday. If I go abroad I tend to try and bring something back to remember my holiday by, and that was I think my first holiday abroad. The elephant again, the wicker elephant and s plant in it is just a reminder of another holiday.

SW: They're kind of mementos.

HT: Yes, mementos. You sit here and you suddenly remember the good times you've had on holiday, and it's something to remind you of those times. The plants, big palm plants; something that my husband and I have in common; we look after it, something I bought that was nearly dead and now, some years later it's still living, it's something to care for, to look after.

SW: One thing that interests me, picking up on what you have said, is that here we are sitting in this symbol of modern living and you say the thing you're more drawn towards is a more traditional way of thinking. Do you feel, sitting in this room, that it's had an influence on the way you have organised it? Do you think you have tried to make it look modern in here, or actually are you trying to make it look more olde worlde?

HT: More olde worlde I suppose. Rather than anything, my pictures are my escapes. The pictures I have got, and my oil painting of my grandfather, they are olde worlde I suppose, traditional. I'm not a modern, with-it type of person, and therefore the furniture I've got is my parents'. It's fairly old anyway. I don't try and be modern because the tower block's modern. I just try to create the home atmosphere I want for myself.

SW: Do you go out looking for various objects, or do you somehow just accumulate them?

HT: I accumulate them. The figurines I am looking for, but other things in my travels I have found, or I have just had handed down to me, and I've collected them really. Some of them I had before I came to the flat, but not very many.

SW: Do you think objects merge into one another, even though you've got new things, things you've had for a long time?

HT: I think they all collect into together, I don't think anything really looks out of place. I think they tend to complement my taste; everything is on the same lines, and it does merge in.

Silvia Foskett

Hunter House, Highfields Estate, Feltham, West London.
'Multi-storey Mosaic' Homecourt. June 1980.

SW: What do you think attracts you to them?

SF: I don't know, it's like with everything in here really, we didn't set out to collect anything in particular.

RF: It just happened.

SF: It just happened. We started with the spoons. For instance, when we went to Cornwall about six years ago and I wanted something to say, oh yeah, I had been to Cornwall, and you either had these little souvenir mugs and things . . .
I bought a few of them at first and I thought, 'Oh it would be nice to have a spoon,' and we just started collecting them and everywhere we go I buy a spoon so it's gradually building up.

SW: This spoon collecting, it says something about your . . .

SF: It's a memory, oh yes, definitely. Not so much when they're hanging up, and they're rows of spoons, but when you take them down to clean them, cleaning each one and you think, 'Oh yes, I bought this in Cockington, that's that nice little village in Torquay.' And you remember things about it, or I do anyway, all the different things, the trip to Jersey, and the horse racing at Ascot, and the Christmas at Butlins; they all bring back little memories.

Lizzie Grant
Joanna House, Caroline Estate, Hammersmith, West London. 'Can Two Views Ever Really Co-exist?' October– December 1983.

SW: I mean, do you ever feel isolated here yourself?

LG: If I go into my room, shut the door, yes, because it just seems so far away from the rest of the estate and all it looks upon is a school, nothing else, except the flyover, and then in the distance you can see the other estates which is Kings Mall, so you do feel a bit trapped in that room if you stay in there too long.

SW: But you tried to alter it, didn't you?

LG: Yes, I've done a great big mural of a cat, which I've finished now, finally. I've put blue sky, green and grass and flowers.

SW: Well, why did you do that, why did you make this mural?

LG: Because I wanted something different on my wall from everybody else. I just didn't want plain walls, I didn't want a wall-paper up there, so I decided to do this cat on the wall, 'cos I like cats anyway 'cos they're crafty.

Mr Spiteri

Harvey House, Green Dragon Lane Estate,
Brentford, West London. 'Brentford Towers'.
October–November 1985.

SW: I'm sitting with Mr Spiteri at number 34 Harvey House. If we look around the flat we see that almost everything has been done by yourself. Now, why do you think you got so interested in DIY?

Mr S: I like to make things. I like to see a bit of wood and think, well, that's just a bit of wood and then a couple of hours later, when you've finished the job it's something interesting or something useful and, mostly, if I get bored, if I'm watching the television and there's nothing on the television one evening I'll think, oh I'll go to my box of wood and think what can I make. If I go into a shop and I see something and I think, well, I could easily make that, I keep the idea in my head, come back and make it.

SW: But do you think you need to express yourself through making things?

Mr S: Yes, well, when I've done something and I like the finished job then I'm proud of it and I like it. If something doesn't turn out too good then I break it up; it's got to be right for me.

SW: But you have, you know, created a definite sort of atmosphere here. What sort of atmosphere do you think you've tried to get?

Mr S: Well, really I've tried to make my flat my hobby; I like to make as many things for it as I can. If I see something in a shop and I think, oh, that would look nice in the corner of my flat, rather than buy it I'll try and make it first.

SW: Oh, so you taught yourself everything.

Mr S: Yes, and then I started to collect tools, which at first was getting as many tools as I can, and then about two years ago I got myself a Black & Decker Workmate which has now been stolen. It was down in the shed, somebody stole it, and then about a year ago I got the Black & Decker sort of attachment for making wood dowelling joints and then you can make even better things. This has got lots of dowelling joints in.

SW: This is a table, yes.

Mr S: That thing that holds your shoes, that's got dowelling things right through it. You see, you can drill right through a piece of wood and put a bit of dowelling in and it's not lopsided and it's a good instrument.

Sharon Wood

Harvey House, Green Dragon Lane Estate, Brentford, West London. 'Brentford Towers'. October–November 1985.

SW: You've got quite a few pictures around you, paintings and things like that. Are you interested in paintings or do they remind you of things?

ShW: I've got a lot that I haven't got put up on the walls 'cos we're saving them, but I do like more modern pictures really, sort of. Got some nice ones that are put away. I don't like things that are plain. I like a few things hanging about and the one in the hall with the little message on it, I like things like that. Just a little sentence that means a lot, because that's a little rain in a storm means a lot, 'cos we've had it hard and it's true, it isn't always easy, so I think just a little sentence sums it all up.

SW: But what about, sort of, the pictures. Do they remind you of the outside somehow?

ShW: I think so. I mean, I love the country and all that and to look at them. I think it really puts you into

a dream world because you're in here but when you can look at things like that then it's an escapism really. You can look at things and really imagine you're there. When I look out the window it's as though the world's going by without you. You're indoors in here and you look out and see everybody going to work, or some mums are walking down the road at half eight and I think, well, I'm still in here, and it seems like you're not part of it out there.

SW: What about this wonderful machine here. Does that somehow replace going out or energy that you might use?

ShW: I think it is because usually what I do is get up in the morning, walk down the school, come back and go and pick him up and then that's it for the rest of the day until the weekend, so all I'm doing is my housework, which I can't call exercise, and then I sort of started

putting on weight over the years, well, I was just being a vegetable really I suppose sitting in here doing nothing, watching the tele which bored me to tears, so I did get fat. Now I do five miles a day, or every other day if I'm lazy some days, and it has, I think it helped me to become fitter.

SW: What do you do, you just get on that and do five miles pedalling, so do you think about something else or what?

ShW: No, sometimes I do, I imagine I'm going along the road, 'cos I would like to have a go on a bike on the road. I'd be a bit nervous now, but usually, I might put on a record something like that and that sort of helps you do it or watch the tele, but basically I just get on there and I keep looking at the clock to see how far I've got to go, to get on with it, 'cos like the speedo clocks up the miles and I don't know what I do. I suppose I just sit and think about what I've got to do when I get off it really, start the dinner or whatever. I just get on with it.

SW: You don't ever think, it doesn't occur to you, it might seem a bit funny?

ShW: I did at first. I'm used to it now, I do it in the hall, out of the way, but now I don't care, if someone's here while I'm doing it, I just get on with it. At first I was ever so, I done it in private, and it's the same when I'm doing the exercises as well; it was all in private, but now I don't care, I just do it.

SW: Do you ever feel outside's a sense of unreality, then?

ShW: Yes, I do feel that, everything's going by and you've just stopped still in here, everything's still going on outside. I look out the window as I said. You see everyone walking around and cars driving around and that and you do feel like here you've stopped, the clock's stopped, but there it's still going on. I don't think there's anything.

Linda Hutchinson

Hunter House, Highfields Estate, Feltham, West London.
'From a Walk to the Supermarket'. April–October 1990.

SW: Do you think it makes the place more interesting?

LH: Oh yes, well obviously. People say 'Where did you get that shell from?' or, yeah, it's like a talking point. I could say, well I went to Margate, like I am telling you.

SW: So in a way you could say it's something that facilitated, like an agency, you bounce your mind off it, outside this space . . . So what about the doll? It's very beautifully presented, unquestionably the whole centrepiece of the room. So tell me about this doll, why do you think you were drawn to that doll?

LH: I don't know, I just love that doll. I actually went to this exhibition with the school, my daughter's school, saw the doll there, and I went back the next day because they were making them there, there and then, and I got it, and I just like it.

SW: Do you think it says something about you?

LH: I like dolls and toys and things.

I don't know whether I am escaping back into my childhood, lost childhood, I don't know, I keep thinking that is what it is, I keep buying things like that. Never used to be drawn towards anything like that, but the last couple of years, anything I see that attracts my attention to do with little dolls or toys, I buy it.

SW: If you look at the outside, it's very anonymous. Do you think therefore you have got to do things inside to counteract that?

LH: I think you have to create your own world, your own little life, what you like, what you have to live with. When I first lived here I wasn't really interested in anything like that, it was totally different in here, but over the last few years I have changed, I have just started getting really into things, I don't know like pictures of children, and as I said toys and things, and I just surround myself with it.

SW: But you see there's a lot of these things so they must be your expression of yourself.

LH: They must be, that's what I am saying, because I messed up my childhood I am reverting back into it, kind of relive it now just by buying things. I suppose they are around me to comfort me. The bedroom is the same; it is full of stuffed toys and dolls.

SW: But they are particular kinds of objects, they could easily be different kinds of objects, people do tend to buy objects to see them as an expression. Why these objects, so you think it's got something to do with your childhood?

LH: I do, yes, I never did until recently. As I said, I kept buying things, and I kept thinking why am I buying these things I never used to, like things like this, but now I've bought loads of them, I've bought hundreds of those dolls all different kinds.

SW: Thinking about the way you painted it and arranged all these pictures around, you've got lots and lots of pictures. How do you think you're breaking up the space?

LH: Well, these are plain rooms so, something happened and I thought I want pictures everywhere. But the pictures that I wanted, as I said, were children, as I said all of children, old-fashioned children and sort of ghost children, and things like that, just had this obsession with children and toys, whereas I didn't with my own kids when they were younger, I mean I was a good mother and everything but I don't know, something has changed in me that has made me want all this sort of thing around me.

Ronald Powell

Snowhill House, Snowhill Estate, Bath.
April 1991.

SW: And when you came here what did you try and do, did you try to create an atmosphere, did you start work on the place or . . .?

RP: I'll try and explain the best way I can, which is that it's sort of half and half. If you look around you see like the black vases and black ornaments and it's halfway through I am bringing back furniture to match the room up, I am looking for a cultural Africa sort of look in the place, so half of what was here before I came along has gone out. My girlfriend and I are throwing things out in order to create an overall effect, so it's rather weird-looking now I think.

SW: So you are trying to bring into it a special African feeling to the place.

RP: Very cultural like, you know, for anybody who walks through the front door it has got to be real comfortable, so you can relax and so on. That's what I want, cosy little spot. If it's raining outside I can put my feet up and relax.

SW: What interested me was you were saying you were bringing in all these black objects and things. Are there some objects that mean quite a lot to you?

RP: If I look at any object here it tells a story. That elephant figure over there, that is very dear to me in a way, if you notice the tusks, real ivory but I pulled them out, simply because I didn't like that, it looks a bit weird without the tusk but still. Each time I looked at it with the tusks on it created a little bit of a conflict between me, that it came from a real live animal, so with it as it is now I feel more at peace with it. Strange feeling that. As for the overall look, it's got a lot to do with my past, my black past. I like to picture power to people who live and pass on, Luther King . . . and Malcolm X. People when they come in they say 10-13 Ah!

They could have a read you know, give them that bit more information the person that's lived and so on. You watch the TV and you see a five – or ten-second clip on a particular person, and they only go so far.

SW: So what you want to do is to develop a kind of information bank.

RP: That's got a lot to do with it. I've got a friend who actually printed that material for me on the wall.

SW: So you're going to make a mural on the wall.

RP: Exactly . . . This spot here and it's amazing people come around they look around the walls. You walk into your best friend's house or a neighbour's house, and you look at the wall and you say 'Oh, that's very nice,' you don't look at the stereo or anything else. Something that catches your eye you know.

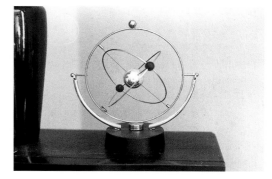

Mike and Mandy Benson

Kelson House, Samuda Estate, Isle of Dogs, East London.
'Personal Islands'. February 1993.

SW: What did you set about doing, what sort of atmosphere did you try to create in here, do you think?

MaB: Harmony. Harmony and . . .

MiB: Cottagey.

MaB: . . . Yeah and we wanted to bring like the outside in, like plants and make it all countrified and that type of thing.

MiB: You know, we put the flowered curtains up and the lead-like windows up there to make it have a kind of country feel and that was our aim, to cheer the place up and make it nice and colourful. And we are high up and it's very hard to get out of the block, the lifts break down quite often and it's not just simple like walking out your street door and you've got fresh air. It's quite a nuisance going out so we had to bring the outside in, in a way.

MiB: We've also got Egyptian kind of things and we've got a lot of religious plaques and that's because we're Christians and we've got this affinity with that kind of life, Egyptian and Greek and like easterly sort of spiritual, kind of philosophical . . .

SW: Does that affect your life in the flat or not, or is it something more?

MiB: Well, they're only objects, but they do make you feel a little bit more happy and you look at, you look at an Egyptian plaque for Tutankamen or someone and you can think back years ago and it just brings nice visions to your mind.

MaB: Yeah, you get a comfort from them . . .

MiB: . . . You get comfort, you think of Jesus and you think of the Old Testament and all the patriarchs, people like Joseph, that went to Egypt and things like that.

SW: So when you're living in the flat, what things do you think . . . I noticed those weights and various things. Are there things that you've got here that compensate for the fact that you can't extend out physically?

MiB: They have actually, yes, because I used to go training three or four times a week and because the hardship of getting to Aldgate and back I've had to bring weights into the house and we're both interested in getting fit, but it's just getting round to it really. I do it quite regularly, but not regularly enough like I used to and that's another thing the block's stopped me doing because it's such an awkward place as well.

SW: So in a way the physicality of the block inhibits you from expressing yourself physically . . .

MaB: We'd like to go jogging and it's just so hard that, you go out jogging, to come back you've got to get in the lift, you're all sweaty and other people are in the lift.

MiB: We did try it before and then we tried mountain bikes, but someone nicked our mountain bikes, and even that was a hardship, getting them in the lifts and getting them in the flat so you're quite restricted to what you can do, so whatever you do you've got to really do it in the flat.

Nick Harrison

Kelson House, Samuda Estate, Isle of Dogs, East London.
'Personal Islands'. February 1993.

NH: . . . when I started working on the flat and I did a fair bit of decorating. A mate of mine on the ninth floor, Paul, helped me with the plastering and some building work and I basically did everything else myself on a limited budget of about two hundred pounds . . . and I bought timber and built shelves, and erm we couldn't afford, I wanted to put tiles on the floor, but couldn't afford tiles so I bought some industrial floor paint and mixed it because it's a red, but the red was too bright so I mixed black into it to make it a darker colour and I've got newspapers on the walls. I just wanted to make the colour and the light of the room to be all sort of harmonious, but pleasant to live in. I wanted it to be pleasant, we're gonna live here and I wanted it to be a pleasant place to live.

SW: Right. I'm interested in your sensibility, you have this paper on the walls, and there's newspaper on the furniture and so on, and it gives it , to my way of thinking, a very sort of ephemeral, transient feel, I mean maybe that reflects your travelling somehow?

NH: Well I put the newspaper, I got the Pravdas and stuff, when I put on the wall from an idea, I saw a Chinese film on the TV, but when the newspaper print, when it's bleached by the light it goes a warm sepia kind of colour and it's quite a warm quality about it which makes it actually quite nice, it makes it quite pleasant, but when I was travelling, although I didn't know it before I went travelling, there's a lot of places in Asia where they actually do use newspapers to put on the walls because they don't, they can't afford wallpaper, or it's not manufactured in certain areas of the world, they don't have it . . .

SW: So in a way do you think this flat reflects your travels?

NH: To a limited extent, I didn't want to. I've been to people's houses and they've been travelling and every inch of the flat is covered with everything that they've bought when they've been travelling and it's I mean I was travelling and it was quite an experience, but I didn't want to try to retain that feeling when I was back here, I mean this is not India or Asia, it is my own flat so I've got a few, I've got two, a textile, one piece of textile hanging on the wall, which is a particular one that I like and then there's the newsprints and the newspapers that I collected when I was travelling but I'm more interested in the fact that they are different typefaces. Because I studied graphics I'm interested in the different typefaces that they use and the styles of lettering that they use from different languages.

Paul McGarr

Top Mast Point, Isle of Dogs, East London.
'Personal Islands'. February 1993.

SW: That's fascinating, so in a way the outside world is distant from you.

PM: No, no, no, not distant, the outside world in the immediate sense of the immediate locality, it's not distant it's like you hop over it in some ways, and the outside world, partly because of the work I do and also the social context, I was very close and being here reinforces that because when I look out there for instance, then I can see the blocks where people that I know live, and even though they may be three, four miles away, because I can physically see them, which is unusual for living in London, in a sense that brings them that much closer. I can give you an example. There's a block that's about three miles away where a close friend of mine lives. Because you can physically see them, not them personally but the building, this person lives there and you can identify physically where you know people, that brings that much closer, but in a sense that's at the expense of jumping over the immediate environment.

SW: Are there sort of activities here which extend you away from the physicality of the building, enlarge your psychological realm?

PM: Most of the things for me personally that I do is listen to music and reading, the main things that take me outside of the immediate world around you. The cooking serves a very practical purpose, psychologically that's because of the work I do. Most of the time I'm reading, writing, thinking, concentrated mental work, whereas cooking's a good way to switch off, and it's marginally physical to do something with your hands, you know, close your mind off.

Henry Elba

Fenton House, Heston Farm Estate, Heston.
'Private Journeys'. May 1994.

HE: I meet a lot of people, a lot of pressure and it's always nice to come home to this living room without nobody to put any unnecessary pressure on you.

SW: So you feel you can shut yourself off.

HE: It is because you will find the most occasions you need that free time to yourself, everybody need that time of relaxation as a way to isolate oneself, because it gives you room to breathe, to think things out, because you're under a lot of pressure from the moment you walk outside. There's so many people that knows me, and there's so many work that I do, so many different types of people that constantly keeps you thinking all the time and when you come here, time, time for me is to relax, a living room is a time to relax, put your feet up, read a book and to be able to concentrate on life in general.

SW: Is there a kind of atmosphere that you've consciously tried to create in here, in this room or is it something that's just come about at an ad hoc level?

HE: When you use the expression 'atmosphere', most areas, a house is only a haven when you have people in it, you must agree, but actually, the atmosphere you actually got here is one where you shut yourself off from the environment round you as I said to you earlier and I'm more of this country guy, I'd rather live in the country, where literally I can relate myself thoroughly, where there's no one around. There's always time when you need to go out and meet people, i.e. like Saturday night to have a few friends round, to do things together and to be with people, also you need that time to yourself, where you can get away, and at present this will have to do, the living room here in Fenton House.

SW: Coming back to this room at the moment there are various things that I noticed, for instance, these executive objects for the desk. What meaning do they have for you? Like this one, I don't know how to describe it really.

HE: It's a form of earth system, well, you'll find many executives have things like that to keep them aware of things around them, but at the same time there's a beauty and a simplicity that these products actually have, at the same time it is something that makes you relax because the work I do involves a lot of stress and a lot of pressure so just looking at these things, just relax the body system, you know, each one of us . . . some people go to a massage parlour or what have you.

  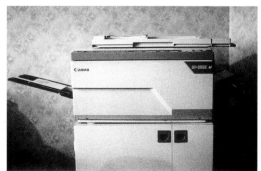

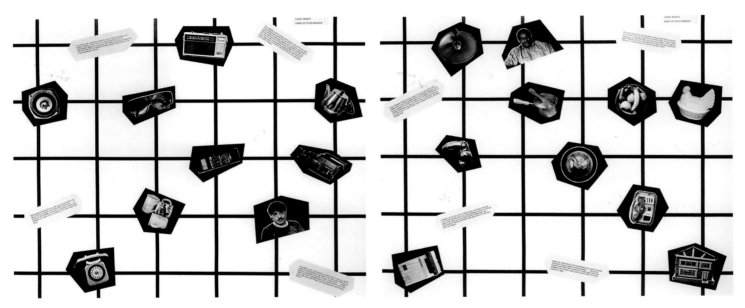

'Living Mosaic', Snowhill Estate, Bath, 1991. Artwork for two of four display boards made with residents of the estate.

Extended space

'Living Mosaic', Snowhill Estate, Bath, 1991. Display board situated in the foyer of the central tower block.

The exhibition of order and control by a higher authority was fully expressed and implanted into the inhabitants of those modernist municipal housing estate environments that proliferated during the 1960s and early 1970s. Especially for children, though true for all age groups in different ways, the immediate environment beyond their flat became a necessary extension, a territory to use, but for this to happen it had to be symbolically transformed, to be socially and psychologically possessed.

Writings, drawings, interventions into the invariably concrete fabric as traces of psychologically transforming moments, these not only radiate a message of identity and society but of the creative potential of the individual. As a result the expression of people's lives on the estate is an entropic force that eats away at the utopian order projected and imposed in the 'plan'. The enlargement of personal and community space, by the inclusion of abandoned and unlikely places into one's own sphere, can be a psychological projection, a cognitive reading of space that transforms in the mind what is encountered or fixed in a landscape, forming it into a personal framework of references that connects it up to what is already established as one's own. I particularly noticed this cognitive enlargement of personal space when working with people who were in a fixed, confined space, such as at the office desk, or in a physically small and isolated flat, such as at the top of a tower block. Often objects people owned agencied an enlargement of the space possessed by them, and in the case of residents of high-rise flats, gave them a connection to something in the landscape they could see from their window, which could then be included in their personal realm. This transformation of exterior space, the estate environment, so that it could be psychologically possessed, gave an area of attention to a number of works of mine, in particular the 'Berlin Wall Drawings', 1980 series; Brentford Tower, 1986; and 'Personal Islands', 1992.

'Personal Islands'. Installation in the foyer of Kelson House on the Samuda Estate, Isle of Dogs, 1992.

'Living Mosaic', Snowhill Estate, Bath, 1991. The 'mosaic grid', on which people's responses to questions were shown on five display boards, was situated on a spot in the estate where residents normally congregated.

A view of the space under one of the buildings in the Märkisches Viertel, North Berlin.

A typical facility provided by planned environments for extending space. This play area on the Avondale Estate, Hayes, West London was never used and lay abandoned.

Children of the Märkisches Viertel

At Märkisches Viertel, at Frau Jakob's flat
Wesendorferstrasse 6, Berlin.
'Berlin Wall Drawings'. 1980.

Märkisches Viertel, North Berlin

SW: So, what kinds of things do you do then, I mean, around here if there is nowhere to play?

Child: Völkerball. Mostly we play ball. Last time the caretaker grumbled again that we weren't allowed to play here, the old people only complained. When we roller-skate down the slope, it's just the same: an old woman grumbles again. It's very bad here.

Child: We draw squares and play, and as she said, then comes the caretaker, and when we play on the playgrounds on the climbing frame, perhaps in the afternoon, the old people shout down to us and sometimes get the caretaker.

SW: Can you tell me why you do these drawings?

Child: At least nobody grumbles at us making them.

Child: Because nobody sees us.

Child: Besides, the tenants don't care at all about the houses and how they look, they piss in the corners or break bottles, and everything stays, and the caretaker isn't the best either.

SW: Tell me about a drawing you did, describe it a little.

Child: I drew a face with long hair from the side, it was a picture of Claudia, and I wrote underneath 'Claudia', and they put over pebble dashing so that you wouldn't see it because they were sour about it.

SW: Why did you do that?

Child: Because they had drawn a cartoon of me, so I drew a cartoon of her.

SW: Is this almost a kind of game?

Child: Yes, who can tease the others best.

SW: And what drawing did you do?

Child: Well, a head with a long nose, also from the side, and I like drawing warts on it. We always draw that at school, and thus it's much more fun.

SW: And what drawing did you do?

Child: I drew Andreas from the side, and they put over pebble-dashing, too.

SW: But do you always draw faces, do you never draw anything else? What else, for example, did you draw?

Child: Well, we played, and I drew a shopping trolley. But they didn't recognise it.

SW: And what sort of game was that?

Child: Well, someone starts off, and the other has to guess what it is.

SW: Do you think that the drawings you are doing in any way sort of . . . do you think that the drawings you are doing with flowers and so on are related perhaps to the kind of place you might like to live in?

Child: Sometimes?

Child: In most of the cases we do dirty drawings.

SW: But what does it look like when it is a wish? What do you draw then?

Child: I would draw a farm house and a lot of crops.

Child: And I would draw a pretty house and a pretty garden where my auntie is living.

Child: With no walls.

Child: But you couldn't build a house then.

Child: And my granny once confided to me secretly, she said she had scrawled the walls and done lots of mischief.s

Child: But in most cases they don't say anything.

Child: They always say that they were better, even though they made the same mistakes as us

Child: It's the same with the lift and all this, and they say it's children. They sometimes draw at places, eg. where the floor buttons are, 1st floor, 2nd floor, 3rd floor, but they can't reach there, I can just about reach there.

Child: Because it's also youths that draw a lot.

Child: Because so little is done for them. They always do a lot for the older people, but for the youths . . . They do drawing out of boredom.

SW: Do they think that the grown-ups understand them, understand why they do the drawings?

Child: No, 'Why are you doing that? You can't do that!' one has to pay for it all – they always think of money only.

Child: Once I drew on the wall and then I ran away, and suddenly there was a man and a woman standing there, they are walking along. Suddenly this man beats me on my head, I didn't know at all why he was doing it. He hadn't seen me, because I had come around the corner. Suddenly he beats me on my head.

Brian Chaplin

Charville Lane Estate, Hayes, West London.
'Two Worlds Apart'. Charville Lane. September–October 1981.

BC: Well, when we first came here there was nothing going on, but now, well when the Jubilee started up that is when all the activities started. We used to have street-to-street collections for the Jubilee, then we had the family night disco and we asked all the family to come to a disco, we had junior discos, we had mini markets to raise the money for a party, we landed up with nearly a thousand pounds for the Jubilee. We had money left over so we carried on, we had a 'do' at Christmas for the children, Christmas party, we then still had money when we finished that so we carried on again, we had another mini market, a stall in Hayes Park carnival then we had another market, a Christmas market in November.

SW: Yes, how does the mini market work?

BC: Well, it's just stalls, you know. We go round and knock on each door about a fortnight, three weeks beforehand collecting jumble and anything that they like to give us, they have a furniture auction, plants, bedding plants, plenty of bedding plants, loads of them, I bring a lot of the stuff up myself or I go to the nurseries and buy them and then bring them home and rear them up a bit higher and then we sell all the stuff then.

SW: Is it mainly plants then or just bits of old junk?

BC: Well, we have a plant stall, cake stall, tea stall, tombola, jumble, odds and ends, books and toys.

SW: Yes, and they're just things people give you.

BC: Yes, people make up a dozen cakes and give us, or someone'll come out and make the teas and we sell the teas, jumble we just stick it all, we have the women round and sort it out, but the furniture was the good one 'cos we had fridges, oh we had about four fridges, about six lawn mowers and chairs, tables. We sold the lot.

Pat Purdy and Anne Tuffin

Avondale Drive, Avondale Estate, Hayes, West London.
'Pat Purdy and the Glue Sniffers' Camp'.
January–September 1981.

PP: Yes, I don't know what, at one time, we'll see in the bad weather during the winter months we'd, we'd have to hang about here we didn't go over to the fields and we'd hang about on the stairs and the corridors and sit there and freeze to death on the stairs and then you'd just start writing on the stairs, something to do, we'd just sit around on the stairs, slip in the corridors and you'd get somebody coming out saying, get out the corridor and take your dog-ends with you.

AT: So you'd go along to the next block and then someone'd come out.

PP: We'd just wander from block to block around the corridors and sit on the stairs, or sit in the sheds.

AT: Yes, down the sheds.

PP: Down the sheds sit in those hallway places there.

SW: 'Cos a lot of people talk about kids, vandalism, breaking up the estate that's the sort of typical thing older people come up with.

PP: Well, I used to go to youth clubs, especially during the winter months rather than the summer months 'cos we used to be over the fields and I could get out, but the winter months we used to go over to the youth clubs so I wasn't on the estate as much as other people but when I was hanging about on the estate you just sit there and start talking and you got a lot of energy in there, in you that you can't expel anywhere, you sit and you start fidgeting.

AT: Before you know what you're doing you've got a pen sort of.

PP: And then you sort of, you pick something up or start on something, you start scratching into something, it's just nerves and you build up, you've got so much energy to expel and there's nowhere to do it, nowhere to do it.

PP: You're not allowed on the bits of green down there in between the

blocks you're not allowed to play football, the kids aren't allowed to play football on those greens. they've got one green and one green only to play football on, not allowed to play on the little bits of green in between which is controlling us and trying to keep us down, trying to keep the kids down and I'd say if the kids are outside playing, and the way the noise travels around these places you can hear it, the further up you go the louder you can hear it, there's just no break from it all.

AT: The only place we could go really was over the track 'cos you could shout, scream, do what you wanted to do without anyone shouting out the window, 'Shut up!', even out in the park we used to be out there and all kids make a bit of a racket and that but half eight at night and they was shouting out the windows, this is summer when it's light, it's awful, you're really restricted.

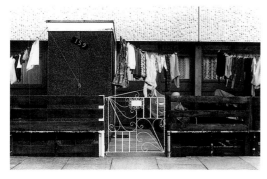

Mrs Edna Muir

Harvey House, Green Dragon Lane Estate, Brentford, West London. 'Brentford Towers'. October–November 1985.

SW: Looking out the window, what sort of things could you see in the view that you found interesting? You mentioned that building.

EM: Now that, I always think of sailing . . . when you go to Portsmouth you get a little boat over to Isle of Wight, now that's only a tiny trip but absolutely fantastic, it is, I love it, and I would like to go on a trip on a boat, a really long one. If we go away for holidays we always take the boats round the harbours and across to another every time, but I think it's because I would like to be on a boat, it's day dreaming again.

SW: Yes, that's what I'm wondering.

EM: I do like to day dream, oh yes, if you haven't got your dreams, you might just as well because it is the day dreaming you do that sort of keeps you going.

SW: So the building reminds you of a boat, then. What part of it actually does remind you of a boat?

EM: It's not exactly the building, the actual building itself, it's how it sort of forms, I suppose the roofing and the chimney and all that from a distance in the background you can only see that part of it sort of along what we would call the horizon. It's not that actual building, it's the one right beyond it, and it looks as if you've got the big funnel and the smaller ones and different things all on it, actually it reminds me of a war-time, like a destroyer, if you can understand the bits and pieces round the side where they've the guns and different things.

SW: The other thing you mentioned was like other flats, you know, sometimes you look out and you look into other flats and things.

EM: Well, I don't say I look into them.

SW: Not like a nosey parker sort of thing.

EM: No, it's just that if you look out the window and the lights are on, I mean I know a lot of people look over to here, 'cos I've actually stood there and watched them, you can see that they're looking over to this part, I've actually seen someone with a pair of binoculars looking, so, it doesn't worry me.

SW: You don't sort of like shout across to each other.

EM: Oh no, no. Half the time I don't think they would hear because right up here when you've got the wind blowing you can't, it's like trying to whistle to somebody down the bottom you wouldn't get them to hear unless you've got someone with one of those big forcible whistles like, you know, you wouldn't be able to hear it, but, oh no, I don't think you can communicate like that, the only thing you can do if you know a person you can sort of wave and get them to wave back, 'cos sometimes the children might look out the window and see somebody at another window and wave their hand, other than that there's no communication at all.

Paul Sheppard

Saffron Court, Snowhill, Bath. 'Living Mosaic'. April 1991.

SW: Are there any focal points on the estate?

PS: The main one is dead opposite my house, actually. There's a chair there and a wall and it tends to be a focal point, for certainly youngsters, until various times of the day, this is the place they meet during the day it will be the parents with their children, they're bringing them along and they all go out there all day when the weather's nice, the telephone box is just down the road from us, people tend to, some of them use it as their own personal phone, it's not very far away from their doors and I suppose these are the main focal points.

Felix Dicam

Aylesford House, Tabard Garden Estate, Staple Street, Southwark, South London. 'Changing Everything'. South London Gallery. July 1998.

SW: One of the other things we filmed was that handle, that was also quite interesting wasn't it, on a door?

FD: I was puzzled by the handle on the door, I couldn't figure out why you'd have a handle which is against the wall by the door rather than on the door. Now what I didn't realise and it's always somebody who is disabled in the house, we came back, we saw a disabled person being deposited out from an ambulance and the person that's using the door and the handle beside the wall as a means to get up. So the handle had a function but it didn't seem obvious at first sight. And the person got up then and went into the house, so a very good reason for why the handle happened to be beside the door, but it struck as something quite out of the ordinary.

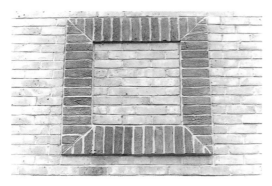

James Gilbert

Farnborough Way, Peckham, South London.
'Changing Everything'. South London Gallery.
July 1998.

SW: So walking on a bit we came across those signs, like a sort of gang sign, they seemed quite articulate, well made. What association did you have with that?

JG: Well, most of the things people do they tend to do for gain, like, this previous poster we saw was ideally for the person who put it up a chance for people to go and pay money and they can walk away and say they've made some money, but that sign is very personal to the person who made it and to this particular set of people, it's something, it's a definite, it's almost like . . . if you look at this at a dog level it's almost like a dog urinating on the wall, it says that this person exists, this is their patch. It doesn't actually say anything about the person at all except that they've done it and only the people that know the individual with that tag

would know them and know what they're capable of, but to a stranger seeing these tags they always seem violent really, there's a violent connotation to graffiti which employs a certain element of fear because it's outside the design which is given by greater authorities, etc. . . . that say that things should look this way. In one way it's quite free because it's imposing upon that rule, but at the same time it's setting a rule of its own but only within that certain subculture or group of people who know that tag.

SW: So are there different signs like that set up all around the estate, different groups?

JG: Yes. . . I think they're called tags, the tags are, it's like having . . . it should be looked upon as the same as having a tag on a piece of clothes. You know, if you pick up a shirt and it had somebody's name written inside it,

you know that belongs to someone, but you wouldn't immediately get any picture of what sort of person they are except by the design of the clothing. But when you see a tag on the wall, to somebody who is not aware of the culture that goes with it, it's quite intimidating. Again, it's outside the established order, outside the authority and it's imposing something which is written in an almost cryptic way. So the language that's used can only be understood by the people who use the tags. So in a way it's quite threatening.

SW: Actually one of the things that we photographed earlier on was a Tennents can, beer can, that was like thrown away.

JG: Thrown away to somewhere in the hope that no one would see it. I'm thinking that the pressure, the controls that people have on their own lives, so that they use

drink or drugs or whatever, to almost like test the will and with alcohol it's like when a person gets to the Tennents stage I suppose there's a certain element of shame because they've lost control of their own power, but that's a part of the reason why they choose that is because they don't feel as though they've got any power in their own life.

SW: So the Tennents is a particular kind of symbolic drink . . .

JG: Yes, it's symbolic of many things, it's legal, it's accepted and yet it's something that in this area in particular you see a lot of men, mainly older men, because of family breakdowns or whatever, end up just spending their days drinking very strong alcohol, with all the problems that will produce.

Sabina Emmanuel

Southampton Way, Peckham, South London. 'Changing Everything'. South London Gallery. July 1998.

SW: There were those sort of like tribal graffiti signs which your son told you about a bit.

SE: Yes, it's the young Peckham boys' sign. It's all over the estate, all over the walls. They put it there to let each other know that they are around. I don't really know, it's just that my son told me what it meant because I just thought it was the kids being stupid putting all this graffiti all over the place and defacing the place, but he said, 'Oh that's a gang, mum, and that's their sign.'

SW: So they don't think of it as defacing, they think of it as actually leaving a sign for other people.

SE: Yes, that's their territory, their patch, they live there.

SW: So do different areas have different signs or . . . ?

SE: I think so, I'm not sure. I don't really go into that part of society.

SW: You imagine they might.

SE: Yeah, they would do.

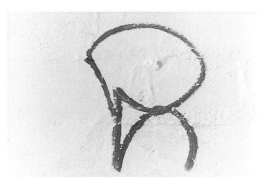

Eartha Davis

Peckham Hill Street, Peckham,
South London. 'Changing Everything'.
South London Gallery. July 1998.

SW: Those cups shoved into the tree. Do you have any associations that you could talk about?

ED: That was more of a tree confined in those metal railings and yet there were these cups just nestled in there. You could treat those cups for passing messages, just ordinary people leaving little notes coming back and finding things or hiding things there. I suppose it sort of brought up childhood images really.

SW: What, like secret places?

ED: Yeah in the middle of all that. You know, the little cups that people buy every day and then you put in little things.

Krystina Stimakovits

Willow Brook Road, Peckham, South London.
'Changing Everything'. South London Gallery.
July 1998.

SW: Do you think those curtains are actually making a display, people behind the curtains?

KS: Yes, I think they make a statement about the people, what's important to them and so I do imagine people who do want to go beyond the normal, or the ordinary, who want a bit more of a statement of class.

SW: Do you think it's in a way sending a message that people want to project themselves out of the environment they're in?

KS: Yes, definitely, so I think in this country it's quite interesting that a lot of very rich people have minimum messages outside on their houses, but quite often poorer people want to give a message of greater wealth or status and it's quite understandable, you try to compensate.

SW: The other thing that we photographed were those long thin windows.

KS: I loved those because of, again, making a pattern, I mean they stay within a pattern but they break it up, they do try and do something different they try to break up the uniformity and sort of the longitudinal thing it's again kind of aspiration, somehow rather than keeping flat they're looking out, they attract your eye towards, to move up, not to stay on the eye level but actually to move up and to look at the buildings or to look at what's beyond the buildings.

SW: They're not really displaying so much about the people inside, are they?

KS: No.

SW: They're trying to hide almost.

KS: Yes, and I didn't get the feeling that it was a private home behind it, so it was more to do with the building, a message about the style of the building itself rather than actually what's inside in a way.

SW: So, coming back to the net curtains, I'm fascinated by this idea that you have that they're a sort of screen. Is that between the conscious and the unconscious to a certain extent?

KS: Yes, definitely and then I think what struck me most were those windows which had a mixture, which were barricaded and then had flowery curtains and then a bit of net curtain, everything, you know, and that almost seems desperate. I mean that gave to me a notion of desperation in terms of anything will do as long as just keep people looking. So there wasn't a concern about what things looked like, all the beauty had disappeared from those people's lives, it was completely functional but in a completely different sense than the thing, it was just function in terms of keeping the outside world out, protection.

'Wie ich meine Fluchtwege Organisiere'. July 1978/May 1980. Four panel work.
Each panel 82.5 cm high x 128 cm wide. Photographic prints, photographic dye,
gouache, Letraset text, ink on card.

Escape

The importance of an actual journey to another space, a space that represented a realm of values and beliefs that were contrary to those that the individual was trapped within became apparent to me when I began working with Frau Hannebauer in Berlin in the late 1970s. The journey to the Schlabergarten from her one-room apartment was a vehicle for the transition from the restrictive determinism of that room to the freedom of nature in her garden. The Schlabergarten was itself a small defined plot, surrounded by high wire fences topped with barbed wire, but the language within that space linked it directly to a wider realm of forest glades, gardens, etc.

With Frau Hannebauer I had the opportunity to talk about the journey and what it meant to close the door on the flat and open the other into the garden. But previously, in the middle 1970s, I had noticed in my work in 'The Lurky Place', a large area of bounded wasteland in Hayes, outer West London, that people had taken objects into the wasteland to facilitate the manifestation of a realm of behaviours and values associated with freedom, identity and community, expressions which they could not adequately externalise in the environments of the surrounding modern housing estates. While the wasteland provided the context in which escape could be realised, the transportation of objects into that context created a means of psychological access; it facilitated the perceptual transformation of reality. I had found all kinds of objects left in 'The Lurky Place' as traces of activities that had gone on there, and they had all at some point been transported through the perimeter fences into that territory. Several years later in the late 1970s when I visited the Avondale Estate that abutted on to 'The Lurky Place' and came to work with Pat Purdy, who had been brought up there,

'The Kids Are in the Streets'. Second triptych. July 1981–May 1982.

Below: The wastelands acted as a context in which pursuits could be enacted as a fantasy. The transportation of an airgun into the wasteland creates a 'hunter'.

Right: Charville Lane residents often used the wasteland to psychologically project themselves into realms associated with situations they could not expect to enter.

I came to realise more and more the symbolic importance the journey had for her in aiding escape. For 'The Lurky Place' was not seen as an extension of personal space, as the immediate environment of the housing block was seen, but as a separate hidden territory; journeying into it, you emphatically left one thing behind to enter another.

At the same time that I was working with Pat Purdy I was also developing a work with Paul Rogers who lived on the Brandon Estate at the Oval, South London, an inner-city environment quite different from that at Hayes. Here the means of escape was achieved through skateboarding, the concrete hills and dips of the skateboard park providing a crucial context for personal expression and community. The skateboard as an object was itself the agent that facilitated a journey from a context of restrictive determinism to one of psychological freedom.

Frau Gertrud Hannebauer

Kaiser Friedrichstrasse, Berlin.
'Wie ich meine Fluchtwege organisiere'.
July 1979/May 1980.

SW: Do you find the enclosed nature of the garden in some way protecting? Does it affect your feelings?

GH: Nature's warmth is surrounding me. I feel protected then. My husband and I used to go for walks quite often, into the woods, that's why nature makes me feel protected in the garden. It's a feeling of cosiness. I really like looking at the flowers next door or at the allotments. My garden is my second home.

SW: Once you mentioned to me you thought the garden was an island. I wonder if you ever felt this just about West Berlin in general, is there a comparison in any way?

GH: The garden is a compensation for living in Berlin. I know we are enclosed here, Berlin is an island and when I go to my garden I am surrounded by nature and can be by myself and this gives me inner peace. I don't feel enclosed concerning the political situation of Berlin. I was born here and have lived here all my life. I, as an elderly lady, do not feel enclosed. I don't get around any more, I haven't even seen the wall yet, as I don't want to see it, I have only seen the wall on TV. It's much easier nowadays for East Berlin visitors to come over to West Berlin. My sister can visit me as well and we can go and visit them over there. This has changed from what it used to be when we weren't allowed to meet at all. The wall is a sad thing but it still doesn't affect me. I don't have to go everywhere at my age and so I don't come across the wall. If I couldn't go any further, I would perhaps notice the enclosure.

Pat Purdy and Anne Tuffin

Avondale Drive, Avondale Estate, Hayes, West London. 'Pat Purdy and the Glue Sniffers' Camp'. January/September 1981.

SW: Can you describe for us now a camp that you built, what did they look like?

PP: It would consist of . . .

AT: . . . them sheets of corrugated iron.

PP: Sheets of corrugated iron that we'd get from the . . .

AT: . . . scrapyard.

PP: Scrapyard, a couple of car seats, we used to try and get the best we could although we used to run over there and just grab whatever's nearest. We used to be a bit fussy and try not to get something too ripped up or in too much of a state, there'd be a couple of double car seats in there, a little, all centred round a little fireplace thing and just the corrugated iron, it's pretty basic but we had somewhere to sit down and we'd try to cover it over as best we could if the weather was a bit dodgy but mainly it was open, I think, I can only remember one that was actually covered over

with the corrugated iron.

SW: What, a sort of roof?

PP: Yes, we used to mainly put the corrugated iron round the sides to block off the wind and block off people seeing us and that.

SW: What kind of objects did you used to take over there?

PP: We didn't take any personal belongings 'cos we couldn't, 'cos it was so open anyone could walk in and take it, we'd just take cigarettes, baked, a tin of baked beans and bread and butter that's about all we'd take over, we didn't take any personal things over and make them into little homes or anything they were just somewhere to go and sit down and have your bread and beans.

SW: But I suppose you would take matches.

PP: Yes, knives, penknives used to go over there 'cos we used to play chicken with the penknives, I can't remember radios over there.

SW: How do you think that place you talk about released tensions on the estate, how do you think that it ever did that?

PP: It got us off of the estate so if we had any little fights or quarrels we could have them over there, you'd get nobody looking out the window saying, stop fighting, stop shouting, stop screaming. We didn't feel that our parents could walk round the corner anytime, 'cos very rarely did our parents come over there looking for us so we didn't feel that they would walk round the corner any minute and find us doing something that, you was . . .

AT: . . . shouldn't do.

SW: But when did you first become aware of it, I mean when did you first start going in there?

PP: When I first heard of it it was always known as the Track and the big lads, the greasers used to go there with their bikes, so I never went near it, I thought it was just for the

big boys. I think there was one summer holiday I went over with a friend, her brother used to go over there so she was allowed to go with him, so I went along one day, we just sat over there and then we started going over there regularly, we sat there watching the blokes riding their bikes and that, and then we started going over there regularly, and then we started to go and build camps, with car seats and that and it all grew on from there.

SW: What would you say would be the age groups of the people that went there?

PP: I was coming up to senior school so I was about eleven then, I suppose it ranged from eleven to sixteen, seventeen, which is the age group that do need something to do round here, the kids round here up to about the age of ten, eleven need to have their parents watching them so they ought to stay on this estate really but over there there's nothing for them to do.

SW: And what kinds of things did ...would you say were the main things that went on there?

PP: Just us building the camps and just strolling around and sitting round talking and smoking and, it's just

mainly set on building the camp and adding bits to it and painting it up and then when we'd done one bit of work, we'd just sit down and have something to eat and just sit there the rest of the day, chatting and talking. It was just a meeting place and somewhere we could relax.

SW: I'm interested in this contrast between this place and that place 'cos they are only like a couple of hundred yards away from each other.

PP: Yes, it's not that far away, I can't really see it from this window I suppose that's why I like it over there so much 'cos I can't see it from this window, the only views I've got from all the windows in the house is of another block that's exactly the same as the one I'm living in and you see someone else looking out the window and it's like looking in a mirror.

SW: Did you used to have territories which you used to kind of defend?

PP: No, we didn't, we all pretty much mucked in together, I'd say, we had about two camps going, I think there was some strange kids, I remember going to the camp one day and it was all broken and battered and somebody had been in there and smashed it up and we never found

out who it was but we happened to find these other camps built that we didn't know about so we moved in there ourselves and moved our gear in and slung the other stuff out and we used it and then I can't remember who it belonged to but we felt it was probably them that broke up our camp so we went and moved into theirs.

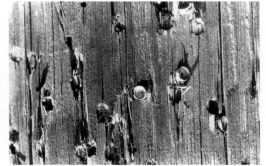

Paul Rogers

Brandon Estate, Oval, South London.
'The Kids are in the Streets'.
July 1981–May 1982.

SW: What do you think they might do, the kids, say they didn't have something like skateboarding to get into, what kind of things do you think they might do or what do you think might happen?

PR: Well, everyone's done it as a kid, you've done things you haven't supposed to do but only because there's, there's not been anything else to do, just pranks really, pranks that can get worse and that like, sort of one prank on a housing estate is to acquire an air rifle and shoot at people from the sixteenth floor or something, that's what I see as not desirable at all, all things with skateboarding, I mean it was never desirable, there was a big outrage when there was like hundreds of people, kids riding along the pavement and that and frightening people and riding into people and that kind of thing so it didn't get off on the right step anyway, I mean it was soon squashed I suppose and

put in the back drawer all ideas of skateboarding but if you don't allow someone to venture out on his own to a certain extent then, he's going to turn against anything you want to give him he's going to turn against anything you want to propose to him whether it be good or bad.

SW: What do you think contributes, then, to the kids just not coming to terms with their own environment?

PR: Well, I really think when things don't work out right you tend to sort of reject it and that's sort of therefore what they do really, I mean take vandalism for example they, they're not actually going out and saying, 'Let's do a bit of vandalism because vandalism costs, costs the council lots of money and makes life miserable for other people,' they don't sort of think about it as that they just think let's go and, let's do this, let's do that, let's kick a window through because we don't, we don't like the set-up,

we don't like what we're getting. They don't know that either themselves really, they're not sort of consciously aware it's just that that's the reaction, that's a natural sort of reaction, they're not even sure, they're not even sure if it's good or bad really.

SW: Yes, if you walked, sorry, if you walk round that estate I mean, we went round the other week, you notice things like the phones are all out of the phone booths.

PR: That's right, yes.

SW: There's quite a lot of devastation around really, isn't there?

PR: Yes, a lot of sort of big windows have been kicked through. There's a window in our block that every time they replace it just gets kicked in, it's crazy but there could be something done about these kinds of places, a bit of paint here and there, a bit of co-operation, well not so much co-operation but the people that live on

the estate direct involvement instead of people that don't even live there, instead of people that live in semi-detached suburban houses with front and back garden making decisions for the people that live on those estates the people that live on the estate should be making decisions for themselves.

SW: You mentioned that skateboarding provided a release from all kinds of tensions, can you elaborate more about that?

PR: Oh yes, well it got me out of the situation where I'd go round to the housing estate where my friends were and just hang about now. We actually had something to do, a new form of transport and great enjoyment, when we got on our skateboards we couldn't vandalise anything, we couldn't take anything out of anything apart from ourselves and our skateboards, that's what, that's what all our energies centred on.

SW: Yes, I mean did you see it as a kind of testing yourself in a way in the real world?

PR: I think it's something like being when the Indian has to go out into the desert and survive, and then come back and he's welcome back in. I see it now as something slightly like that but actually at the time I didn't really think about it too much, all I wanted to think about was my skateboarding and getting, getting out of things.

SW: Did it help, does skateboarding help you face the everyday world, did it make you into a kind of hero like you were able to play out roles like that then?

PR: Yes, well everyone was trying, everyone was trying, trying to better themselves, do well, I mean if there was an exam in it at school, the kids would have passed it with flying colours, it's, trying to explain that is difficult, getting on your own level, you was, you wasn't, you was slightly removed from the rest of the set up, from the rest of life that you were supposed to lead.

SW: Do you think kids do feel more isolated now then in your estate, do you think kids are conscious of that?

PR: No, they're never conscious of their actions really. You can tell a kid a hundred times not to write on the walls but he'll write on the wall, you can tell a kid a hundred times not to smash a window but he'll still

smash a window, it's not a conscious thing, when they're older and they look back at it then they can start to analyse what was wrong, and what can be done for the future, but when they're kids, they could always come up and say: 'Well look, when I was little, people like the social workers and things like that used to come up to us and ask us why we do this and we do that and we'd give them the same old story, oh we're bored and we've nothing to do and there's no parks, there's nowhere to hang about, there's no clubs to go to, all the people telling us not to play football so we play it here and we create just as much noise here', that kind of thing, those kind of answers.

SW: But do you think therefore it's just pure emotion, people are more just emotional at that age, just got emotions that just dictate what they do?

PR: Yes, they're not conscious of it, they're not openly emotional or physically emotional it's just they've got a lot, they've got a lot of, they're troubled but they can't put a finger on what they're troubled by, they can only react to their troubles.

Nicola Astill

Fenton House, Heston Farm Estate, Hayes, West London.
'Private Journeys'. Heston Farm Estate, May 1994.

SW: Well, it struck me like, for instance, when you go through that fence, that hole in the fence. It's like a symbol from one place to another.

NA: It is. It's just a different world. But not just going through that fence, it's just getting out of the concrete, going on to the grass for me is the difference. So I don't have to go into the fields for that. I can walk around on the grass areas around here just to get away from the concrete, but you can always look back and you're reminded of it because you can't get away from these tower blocks, you can see them wherever you are.

SW: Yeah, yeah certainly I can see that. I mean, when we made that journey there were certain things that we looked at, for instance, that blocking up of that space and it seemed to give me the idea that you had quite a strong kind of

history with the place.

NA: Yeah, because you see things like that happening. Well what else can they do about it? They were probably fed up with shouting at people and telling them not to go through their wall and that's what they did in the end. I was quite surprised it was just two blocks. I thought they'd have done it all the way down because you see children will still go through there. That meant something because they put some wood or something there first and that got broken down.

'What Is He Trying to Get At? Where Does He Want to Go?' 1984.
Two-panel work with tower. Each panel 152 cm high x 98 cm wide.
Ten blocks each 44 cm x 20 cm x 20 cm.

Lessons from marginal diversity

I consider that what the generation that grew up in the early 1970s on the 'new reality' housing schemes has managed to achieve is of immense importance to everyone, especially the artist, for they have established their own cultural forms of expression as an overt statement of a counter consciousness based on self-organisation and community.

The catalyst for this explosion of creative forms in the mid-1970s was first hand experience of the deteriorating environment and life in the 'new reality' which directly affected the psychology and identity of young residents stigmatised by their surroundings. These young people were contained, not just physically but socially, and were made to feel by that containment utterly remote from the dominant culture's idealisations that were being constantly projected on to them for emulation. In fact, there was no possibility of emulating those projections for there was neither the economic means nor the psychological will to conform, for the projections had become remote by reflecting a life of possessions that could never be obtained and this generated increasing alienation and hostility. Another focus of this generation's alienation was the further promotion by the dominant culture of a professional identity and the practice of professionalism in areas that had already been rejected by them. This rejection on one hand was directed towards the institutional bureaucracy upon which people were made increasingly dependent, i.e. the various social services, and on the other hand towards the music business, for music was one of the most important catalysts for community feeling. Both, but especially the latter, were by 1975 seen as projecting a distant world that had already become a symbol of alienation. Music had become big business and, instead of being made in accessible clubs by local musicians, was now presented by stars to mass audiences through huge concerts, on elaborately packaged LPs and videos, on TV commercials, all of which tended to elevate the performers into the realms of god-like figures.

Instead of following the projected cultural stereotypes into a reflective passivity as the artists had done, a young generation of residents asserted to anyone, including themselves, that they did indeed exist, even if this had to mean that graffiti and destruction proliferated on the estates. People fought back against their entrapment. What was perceived as wanton vandalism by the authorities can also be seen as an expressed creativity, directed at the context that was most meaningful, the physical fabric of the building in which they lived. The Punk movement, when it first came to public notice, strongly expressed the idea of self-organisation (DIY – Do It Yourself – was an important slogan to Punk) and contextual expression. The Punk ideology was anti-professional, it was for a complete spontaneity, it was also aggressive and alienated, but it expressed a basic mutuality between participants through seeking common languages and common meanings, for now the audience were also the creators.

The fundamental message of Punk that is so culturally important for the artist is that everyone has the potential to express their own creativity, and that what is meaningful to people is relative to the context in which it is received and made. The most well-known form of this DIY spontaneity is through the Punk bands that were formed and the DIY records that they made, but other manifestations were equally important: fanzines, dance and forms of dress and personal adornment. All the different manifestations of self-creativity reinforced in various ways the sense of community for a generation that had been made to feel so culturally isolated, and created a common bond between those that had been so alienated. One way in which this was visually stated to other people was through forms of dress that used codes which were aggressively tangential to the norms of society, and as such they became an important means of denoting independent existence, displaying rejection of the normative world outside the group.

These new DIY codes were created through an important cultural act. Diverse codes and symbols, sometimes with obvious authoritative connotations, were borrowed from the dominant culture, brought together and given a different meaning by being transformed into a new language that reflected the self-identity and sensibility of the creators. Important to these transformations was that the codes and symbols had already been discarded or seen as taboo by the dominant culture, and that bringing them into new original relationships made them an unacceptable challenge to society. The act of simply transporting the codes from social context to social context changed the previously accepted meaning of the codes, and thus they could leave the domain of the dominant culture. The act of transformation is the fundamental act of human creativity, and within our own culture this is shrouded in mystique and often projected as the exclusive preserve of the artist. But for once the whole of society was quickly made aware of the new codes and what they meant by their display on the streets.

While rejecting the norms and beliefs of the dominant culture Punk still had to coexist within it, this dilemma being resolved by establishing, as a natural consequence of their DIY philosophy, its own parallel world of social resources. Thus Punk subsequently evolved over a number of years into a more established foundation of a counter culture, a culture of the night. Agents for communication and centres of community were set up, unlike those of any institutional hierarchy, and with no monolithic permanence, but as a continually changing, self-organising network. Particularly important to this more recent 'night culture' in the 1980s are the 'private clubs', started by individuals from those 'new reality' housing estates, principally for their friends, to create a feeling of community and to screen themselves from the prying eyes of the dominant culture so that they could freely express themselves. The importance of these private clubs as a context or institution is that they were a denial of the property values held by the dominant culture's institutions, for they were started mutually among friends for friends.

The relevance to the artist of these private clubs is that they were there to act as a creative catalyst, to further an origination and expression that would be unacceptable to the prevailing social norms, certainly those dominant in the art museum. The private clubs were institutions of a kind, and as such they were a statement by the night people of their self-organisation, and patterns (in actuality they were opening and closing all the time) and preferences evolved and were altered by those who created them. Here the relationship between the creators of cultural activity and the audience was totally interwoven, simply there was no separation, the audience were participants. This interrelationship between creators, while marginal and without the resources of the dominant culture, nevertheless succeeded in developing a parallel world, and even in intervening in the dominant culture's process of generating new perceptions of itself.

Such an interventional effect was only transient, but the Punks and night people accepted that transience as an essential element to socially based expression.

Note: Extract adapted from Stephen Willats, *Intervention and Audience*. Published by Coracle Press. 1986.

Night capsules

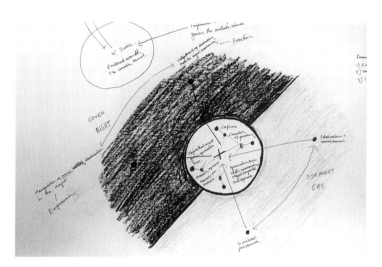

Living Like Goya. Diagram from conceptual model of the definition of Julie Sissons' capsule.

The subcultures that developed in the late 1970s took the creation of personal space within the fixed environment of the 'plan' a stage beyond anything I had previously encountered in the creation of capsulised domains. These were surrogate domains in that they were lived in and inserted into the infrastructure of the housing estate, using whatever was available, but at the same time removing themselves into a distinctly defined internal world. However, this separation, removal, was not a negative outcome, for the new inhabitants vested a fresh creative life into what had become highly stigmatised, bleak and run-down environments. I saw that in the creation of these capsulised worlds, the idea of creative transformation had been taken a step further into an expression of a cultural statement, a total environment. These were transformations from highly anonymous spaces, made without financial resources, reliant instead on ingenuity, lateral thinking and optimistic energy, so giving a very different individual vitality to what they managed to achieve from virtually nothing. They were also transient, temporary installations denoting a moment in the development of an approach to the future. This on-going creativity and fluidity in the definition of total space, on the one hand to hide within but on the other to exhibit individual energy, I saw as fundamental to contemporary traits in culture and as manifesting an important message for approaching its future. Also equally important is the message these interventions have for us, for unlocking the potential of our own creative self-organising behaviours.

*'Private Icons'. August/December 1983. Three-panel work. Each panel
140 cm high x 101 cm wide. Media: photographic prints, acrylic paint,
ink, Letraset text, felt-tip pen and objects found by Tim.
Three mixed media portraits by Tim. Paper on board.*

Garry

Calmer Road, Acton, West London.
'Escape with us into the night'. October/December 1982.

G: Well as I say we're all very black, all very dark people.

SW: What do you mean by that, 'cos I mean you're not black yourself.

G: Oh no, not coloured but everything we like's sort of black, bright things don't really come into our lives, like we're all into different aspects of black, there's definitely the sexual and sort of gothic horror side of black which we all like but there's also the sort of, I suppose sleazy side is the same sort of thing really, but it's night time when we come home from work and we've been sitting round in the daylight all day and the night is just sort of a cover, we are very night people really, we have to go out and put up with everyone during the day, but black just is us, you can use it as a cover, you can use it as whatever you want, people have always been afraid of the dark and I think people have always been afraid of the dark because it's representative of everything taboo; everything taboo always goes on in the dark or in dark rooms or behind closed doors and I prefer that side of life to sort of the everyday, routine, run of the mill sit at a desk type thing.

SW: Do you get a sense of freedom in that kind of context you know – dark?

G: Yes, I feel more myself. I mean during the day you've got, everything's artificial you know, everyone's just going around, living their lives how everyone expects them to be and during the night sort of a different side of you comes out, you can be yourself, you can use the night as a cloak and you can hide away in corners or use it as just a background, that's what we do basically and everything being so black around us then the night is our ideal time, I mean it must be great being a vampire.

SW: Take this environment here, I mean, how do you see this environment, the room we're sitting in and the objects and all that?

G: Well, this is the best we can do with what we've got. I'd love to have the walls black but being a rented place we can't but, you know, if we could just get the walls black, all the black bits and pieces that I call Liz's Biba stuff, all the black leather and studs on the wall, everything like that, and I'd just love the room to be ours so I could do more with it, I mean, it looks okay as it is now, I mean, it still has an effect on people, but not as much of an effect as I'd like.

SW: I was just trying to get the ambience that you feel, the atmosphere that comes out of the room, what do you think you're trying to create?

G: Well, with both of us, both Liz and I living here we've got sort of a cross current, I mean Liz, is more of the decadent twenties air which she likes whereas I prefer more of a sort of violent atmosphere to come out of the room, which is what the leather and that gives it, that little edge but sort of there's not room to have all the skulls and everything, you know, the black candles and the skulls that are in the other room in here and, I'd just like more of a gothic horror atmosphere to come out, out of the room.

SW: What about people's reactions to you locally, people living around you?

G: Well, we don't spend a lot of time, we don't see a lot of the people around here, when we're actually here we spend a lot of the time in the flat, nip out to the shops to get a pint of milk or something, but the people downstairs are great, they like us but they had a reputation for being noisy and not fitting in with the neighbours anyway.

SW: But when you look out the window what do you see you know?

G: Just general boredom, everyone's

just going around living their dull little lives, they live in dull houses, they're not being themselves well, perhaps they are perhaps most people are generally dull and boring, but you look out of the window and you see these row upon row of houses and they all look the same and the people come out in the morning and they all look the same and they all go to work and they all sit there behind their desks in their offices that all look the same, you don't seem to get any individuality at all in the everyday life it's just dead. I like people that are going to express themselves, be what they want.
SW: How do you feel about the products of society like cars, television and all that kind of stuff?
G: I hate TV, I'll say I hate TV but I'll sit there and watch it but it's such a killer, you sit there and it's plonked in the corner and every house has got a TV in the corner and it's the centre of attention and they don't talk; everyone just sits glued to the TV.
SW: What I was referring to really is our consumer society.
G: It's all artificial, it's so, so artificial, but there again people probably say that about my life style, they probably say it's all artificial, it's all a pose, it's all an act. Perhaps it is. Perhaps in a few years' time my views will change, I can't see that happening myself, people keep telling me, I mean people have been telling me for God knows how many years, 'Oh, it's only a phase, you'll grow out of it.'

Liz

Calmer Road, Acton,
West London.
'Escape with us into
the night'.
October/December 1982.

SW: You all seem to like the idea of black, and the idea of sort of like gothic culture.

L: Well, I've worn, I've worn black virtually as far, as long as I can remember not all black, but the last three or so years I've always worn all black, you very rarely see me in colours, I only wear colours just to surprise people basically, and it goes with everything I like, I'm mad on Biba just the fact that it's black and glossy, there's something so sexual about black, black leather, studs, everything you want to do you can do in black far better than you can in, colour is, is more garish it's more, it's cheaper, with black you can create any illusion you want to.

SW: But going back to that flat and that room, they definitely had a sort of atmosphere in there. What sort of atmosphere do you think was going on in there?

L: Well, with my room it's definitely a half and half atmosphere, it's somewhat my personality, my room, because half of it is feminine and Victorian, bits of lace everywhere and Biba bottles and all Biba make-up and everything, everything covered in black, black drapery, sort of an envelope you can close around you and half of it is black studs, black leather, bondage, but it envelops both ends, the aggressive, the sexual side of it and the more, the more, not feminine, feminine's too prissy a way of describing it, the more elegant side of black, the richer, the more powerful side of it.

SW: I mean do you think you were aggressive about what?

L: Well, I'm aggressive about people all doing the same thing, even just stupid things like loyalty to your work. Work owes you nothing, you simply go there and do your job and go home, and people who live for work unless they're the head of a company and amassing fortunes, it surprises me just how naive people are, the way they fit into their little boxes and they never even try to break out of them, so to me it's, it's a matter of trying to break out of the little boxes everyone tries to put you in, trying to be something as such the only way you can do that is by making some sort of strong, especially visual image and the way you live your life must be different so that you are not being stereotyped.

SW: I mean there's self-organisation like you kind of, yes, I suppose it's about self-organisation.

L: A matter of trying to live a community within a community, its definitely a subculture, it's not very large, and everyone helps everybody else, it's a matter of immediate identification and belonging, it's a club that is on the street all the time, in other words, you are a permanent member of that club as you look a certain way, so people will always help you out and you tend to live round people in various spheres you exist together very much, especially our little community in the flat, we lived with each other's, they, in everything, sort of more than a family does, far more, more of a family than your average nuclear family is, and the same way with all of us.

SW: I, well, going back to the night then, just make some relationships for me between the day and the night and contrast them.

L: Well, apart from the visual contrast, the fact that during the day I'm almost, quite acceptable even though I wear floor-length coats and little caps, I mean, I haven't got all my make-up on and my hair's not up, I haven't got masses of jewellery on, but at night I, I look completely different, it's more than that it's a matter of, daylight is so garish, everything is shown up to be filthy and mucky, and so suburban, it's all there stark, whereas at night everything's softer, if there's rubbish in corners it still looks nice at night, it's, it's the same way that you go into a bright room and if you put the dimmer switch on a light the whole room glows and it's a comfortable feeling it's the only time you can feel at home and, night, during the day, you're existing within a vacuum, you're just wandering along and muddling through, it's only at night you can open the door and come out, and feel at home and, definitely, there's the day it's the fact that everything is lighted up and I don't even like light, if I'm in a room I like to dim the lights, I like to put a, an orange light on, I like good light perhaps if I'm working but the idea of a bright desert island is not exactly my idea of bliss.

Scarlett

Tottenham Hale, North London.
'Taboo Housing Estate'. October 1982.

S: You're brought up, and your tastes are supposed to be like this, like you're brought up and your mother wants you to have the same tastes as she does and therefore most people generally their living room resembles their mother's, perhaps it might be a little bit trendier or younger but it does resemble their mother's and this just doesn't at all, I just like red, it reminds me of a womb this room that's why I like it.

SW: What, you're trying to make it like that?

S: No, I just like red, I just always wanted a red room, always and everyone said to me, if you have a red room it's supposed to be very dangerous and you won't be able to sit in there very long and it gives you headaches, well, this is actually my favourite room of the whole flat, just 'cos it's very comfortable, it does remind me of a brain or a womb or something very warm and pumping inside your body that's actually sort of living and it's just, it's comfy.

SW: What you feel comfortable?
S: Yes, definitely.
SW: But I mean do you think it expresses something about you?
S: In a way, yes, 'cos it's something that I always wanted to do which is why I did it. The number of people that say, you know, 'That room is disgusting,' or, 'How could you live there?', but the thing is I can actually live here very comfortably and so in that way I think, yes, it does because it's something that I like, I mean it's not something that I've said: 'All right, because everyone is saying, you won't like it, I've got to say that I like it,' I mean I do actually like it.
SW: But what about the objects, where do you get the objects from?
S: I find them. What did I buy? Nothing. Oh yes I did, bought that red plant pot and that's the only thing I bought in this whole room, everything I find, I find things on skips, I found nearly everything in this whole flat on the skip, this sofa I found in Earls Court when I was up there I found it on a skip, I found that, the table, the record player somebody gave me, I found the chair, I found the ashtrays, I found that chair, I found my bed, I found the cupboard.

SW: Tell us a bit about your life here.
S: About living on my own, well, I quite like it actually. When I first moved in I hated it 'cos I hated living here and I hated living on my own 'cos I'd never lived on my own before, but fortunately I have a dog which takes my mind off a lot of things and compensates for a person and also it's 'cos I lived very differently to other people because I'm up most of the night and sleep most of the day so other people around me don't really affect me very much at all because they're not up when I'm up.

SW: So you just go sniffing around.
S: Well, there's brilliant skips that's one good thing about living around here 'cos, because it's like new and trendy they're trying to keep it very clean and nice and they don't like people dumping large pieces of furniture outside on the rubbish bins outside, so they, they provide skips at the end of every street and people just, people throw out really brilliant things and they always tend to throw them out during the day so that everyone can see that they're throwing out something that really isn't necessary to throw out because they've got a new one or, they've got to be one better than everybody else so I just run along and pick it all up behind them and paint it.

SW: Do you feel more creative at night?
S: Yes, I get inspired to do things, even if I haven't got any money, if I've got a tin of red paint and something that needs painting or something that I think will, I'll just do this and splash about, even if I've got no money I can always find

something to do at night, 'cos like I say you can always just get something, or even I just get something I've been meaning to do for ages and just sort of do them, like this entire room, I mean, I moved in, I painted the room, the room was red and the sofa was red and the chair was red, and that's about it and I really did want everything to be red and I was, 'cos I was working when I was doing the club and I was really busy and then one night I just had a fit, I had absolutely no money and I didn't go out for about the next two days so I just went out and got the tin of paint and just had a fit on the room.

SW: This room it's like a kind of capsule isn't it?

S: Definitely, it's quite nice like that 'cos you can come in and you feel really sort of safe, it's all warm and safe and no one can touch me when I'm in here, it's like a sort of shell really, I feel that if anything happened, anything at all like the world could

blow up and I'd still be sitting here in my little room, with the dog and my cats.

SW: But do you think you can sort of like hide in the night as well?

S: Definitely, yes, because you can literally hide, you can literally hide from the people you don't want to see, you can literally hide from people because people tend to think that they won't phone you during that time, so if you don't want to speak to somebody and they don't actually know you that well, if it's really someone that you don't want to talk to and they're not going to phone you before sort of three or four in the afternoon then, it's okay because they're certainly not going to ring me up at two o'clock in the morning for fear of waking you up, and that's another good thing really, I mean, I usually get all the phone calls in during the day whether it gets me out of bed or not doesn't really make any odds if people need to call me they can call, but I mean it's

quite good because you have actually got something to do and I'm indoors doing it; it means that nobody rings me up and interrupts me, so I can concentrate better.

SW: Do you associate the daylight with just sort of general boredom, or general life?

S: Yes, general life, general boredom, definitely, general boredom, I mean I can get up at nine o'clock go out do the shopping, come home, there'll be no money left, I'll sit here all day and I'll do absolutely nothing just, nothing, I'll just sit here in front of the television watching afternoon TV programmes.

SW: But you did do some extraordinary things like you made that voodoo head.

S: Yes, I mean I just do things like that, I just have a whim, a whim to do things, it's like I decorated this, I mean it was just a plain white blind and I didn't really want to paint it but I suddenly had this whim to whip out

the paint and do a few splashes, and just little things like that, just, all sorts of things, if I'm interested in something at the time then I'll do it there and then I can't bear to put anything off anyway, unless I don't really want to do it, if there's something that I want to do I'd rather travel six miles to go and buy some equipment that I might need to do it and do it that day rather than wait till the next day, I just can't bear waiting for things, I'm just a very impulsive person, I have to do things on impulse, and I think that's how you create things, whether it's from like writing somebody a letter, a sort of exciting, creative letter or like something like the doll, if you don't do things on impulse you don't get anything done, and obviously, with bigger things you have to sit down and think, right, how am I going to do it? But you get this impulse to do something and you think, right, I'm going to do that, and you go from there. I think everybody does but people don't realise it, it's just 'cos I do everything very boldly, and that's why other people notice it more.

SW: Why do you think you do it very boldly?

S: 'Cos I'm a bold person, that's all I'm just a very bold person, I like to be bold about things, I don't like to do things by halves because I like to be bold I just boldly step in, risk my life, literally, practically, also I campaign at night, I get my what's it sorted out, my leaflets, so I can go out leafleting which I don't do very often 'cos I think it's a bit sort of like selling raffle tickets, but then if I do actually think something's important enough I'll do it, the night's a good time for thinking about those things and just sorting things out, I mean, I see people quite a lot during the night, much the same as I would if I saw people during the day, 'cos like I say people I know tend to be on the dole and tend to be up till about three and four in the morning anyway.

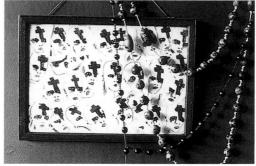

John

Sandridge Court, Queens Drive, North London.
'Difficult Boy in a Concrete Block'. July/November 1983.

SW: They really want social conformity.

J: Well, yes, I think that's what it is.

SW: But you don't want that, do you?

J: I don't want anything that's anywhere near that, I like the idea of not being part of society, I have no wish to work at all, I don't see why I should, what, why the hell should I, I'm not going to enjoy it, I mean if I'm going to do something that I enjoy then that's not what I'm going to call work, 'cos then it's not work, is it? If you enjoy it, then I don't think you can say work, 'cos work is sort of something which you have to do to make a living, whereas I think if you're doing something like you're doing, which is something that you really like doing it's not really work, well say not the straight definition of the term 'work'.

SW: Well, I don't know. How do you get any money then, I mean to do things?

J: I don't know really, I really don't know, I mean I do actually try and work out where I get money from but, I suppose I scrounge it a lot off people and like I just borrow money and, I mean we owe quite a lot of rent but that's no problem, 'cos you just if you get notice of arrears you just pay it, you know, they don't really care, I mean even if you just pay it once every six months, so long as they get it they're not bothered really, so I mean I don't really care, but I mean to me, I mean the only point of having a flat is so that you can go out and enjoy yourself, that's the whole point of living is to have a good time I mean, 'cos it's such a fucking shitty world basically, I mean that is no sort of life for you really, at all, if you just carry on, I mean what I am supposed to do is go out and get a nine-to-five job, so if I get a nine-to-five job I won't

have any time to go out in the evenings 'cos I'll be too tired so what, I'm just going to end up, like I'll be spending all my money on things like vacuum cleaners and colour TVs and things like that which is a load of crap really, I just don't want it, I'd much rather go out and get pissed every night.

  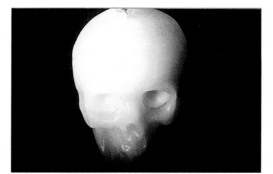

Tim

Quernmore Road, Finsbury Park, North London.
'Private Icons'. August/December 1983.

T: To describe it, I'd just say it's not a very large or nicely proportioned room particularly, and the walls have been covered in silk curtains and I was trying to get lots of reds and, curtains and things at jumble sales, sort of junk heaps and so on and on top of them are pictures, it's like an accumulation of things, layers, like you don't hardly see anything of the walls, I think there's a little place round this side there which has got no curtains on, hanging up against the walls, but on top of them are pictures hanging on top of the curtains, just like say in an old house in a, sort of seventeenth century they'd have tapestries with pictures hanging on top of them, it's a kind of imitation of that, and all the surfaces have arrangements of objects on them sort of vases of plastic flowers, dusty plastic flowers, and sort of statues flanking pictures, a bit like a garniture of vases and clocks and things but instead it's plastic flowers and pictures.

SW: But these objects, and this particular room, what does it mean for you? You've made it in a very particular way, why do you think you've got these objects here?

T: It's a question of surrounding myself with things which I particularly like and ordering them in a certain way, I like arranging things, the fact is this room is very far remote from what's going on outside and you can like close it off, be like enclosed in it, I mean all the hangings and things, the whole sort of, I mean, the entire ensemble as it were which it is conceived in a sense of one really, it's not bits and pieces, I don't like the idea of, the complete idea, all these things are subordinate to the main idea, the idea of this room, if you took things out I think it would be the same, I'm always adding things to it.

SW: What do you think is the central thing that you're trying to create here for yourself?

T: I think a little shrine I suppose, but to what I don't know.

SW: But do you see it as a sort of expression of your own sensibility, it's an expression of yourself?

T: Yes, and my interests, all my sort of particular obsessions. It's a very formal sort of place, it's not a place I don't want anyone else to come into, it's a place where I quite like having people in, and it's for other people to look at as much as it is for me really, it's a kind of like an altar or it's a sort of shrine, an ensemble of things all put together, I suppose, it's definitely for show as well as for myself.

SW: But you feel it's very separate from the world around you. Do you feel very separate yourself from that world?

T: I do and I don't. I mean I, I don't think I live in a different age, or I don't sort of live in a kind of dream world of, I do face a certain amount of reality but on the other hand many people say I do view the world through tinted spectacles, I certainly wouldn't say I was an outsider.

SW: Can you describe how you came to collect these objects, I mean why this particular collection, what underlies all these bringing together of objects?

T: A lot of them I collected just because I like nineteenth-century religious art which is basically unchanged up till about the 1950s. I mean these little statues and those little oleographs and so on, I mean whatever date they are they're basically nineteenth-century.

SW: There's a fundamental preoccupation with religion and death, isn't there?

T: Oh yes.

SW: Well, I mean what gets you involved in this?

T: Where I went to school, my family, both of those I think are quite important, I think Catholicism is quite obsessed with those things anyway, images, and death, and I'm quite interested in that, I'm very interested in that I like the idea, I like the whole sugariness and kind of morbidness of a lot of the religious stuff, and the portraits of popes because it's like a symbol of power with all their trappings, sort of archaic little dolls really with all those tiaras and things on, just mass-produced images, aren't they really? Most of them are, the other things picked up from cemeteries or those skulls over there I collected them when I was quite young, I discovered them in a box, I like bones.

SW: They're like taboo things aren't they, just to have around?

T: I'm definitely fascinated with the things around and the idea of having things which people don't usually want, would prefer not to have inside their house, like those little stones there.

SW: Do you see your paintings as a creative expression?

T: Yes, I do think they're creative. I used to have this thing that they're just fakes and I used to have this bravado kind of, 'Oh, I don't really care very much for them I just do them as a rather kind of mechanical exercise just for decoration things,' but they are actually more than that 'cos I am quite fond of them and I do take quite a lot of care of them, especially now, I'm taking much more care of them.

SW: Do they feel like they sort of release tensions?

T: Yes, definitely, although quite often if I'm under pressure I'll do it like a picture, I mean at the end of it I'll feel absolutely exhausted but at the same time it does release a certain kind of creative energy or whatever, I get quite absorbed in it as well, and I will take a great deal of time on things if I want to, I mean recently I've just spent quite a lot of time on that picture downstairs that's for someone else, I suppose I did it even better than I would do for myself really.

SW: This whole room, you know, in a sense, not only the paintings, but all the objects and so on, seems to be releasing some sort of emotions.

T: I'm always rearranging it and it's really quite satisfying to rearrange and change and at the moment I get quite annoyed because I haven't painted it underneath these hangings 'cos they should be, and like the ceiling I feel it should be, and I feel as soon as I do it and I just want some more flowers or I don't have the right objects to sort of juxtapose, I get quite annoyed.

SW: Yes, funereal kind of things. What attracted you, is it, you know, that it's sort of taboo or, in most people's kind of lives or what?

T: There is something quite taboo about it, I like sort of morbid things, I think it's a kind of trap, I think it's something which I first really rejected, because I mean when I was small I was always told that little plaster statues of saints were hideous and I remember writing things at school talking about the tawdry sort of madonnas and things like that which used to be around the school and I really used to be quite sort of promiscuous in heaping contempt on them.

  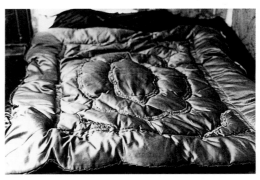

Leigh Bowery

Farrell House, Watney Estate, East London.
'What is he trying to get at? Where does he want to go?'
February/July 1984.

SW: Going back to this place, where we started from, what sort of atmosphere do you think you're trying to create here?

LB: Well, sort of like as a joke we've told everyone we've moved into our luxury apartment, and we started looking at carpets and we saw this really sort of gross shag pile but it was dreadfully expensive, it was like eight pounds a metre or something a square foot, some ridiculous price, so we got the next one that we found which was a really beautiful fun fur which has got sort of black roots and silver ends which is really long and I can do the whole flat for like a hundred pounds, I mean every room and I even made allowances for when I do my bedroom to do the walls as well, so I mean that's much cheaper but it will sort of give a very luxurious though a bit horrible, I mean, sort of like a

send up of a luxurious flat. I do want to be comfortable at the same time so, 'cos I get, I do get like strong feelings from like wherever I am, sort of the environment I'm in, if it's comfortable I can work here, like it's all the better for me.

SW: So, I mean, it's got to have a duallistic function then.

LB: Well, I don't really see the difference, I mean I'm working all the time, even when I'm just like sitting down watching television. I don't sit down and watch television that often but I'll always be like stitching something even if it's, you know, something I'm going to wear that night, I don't see the big definition between work and just living, you could say it's like work all the time but it doesn't seem like that to me.

SW: But it will be like reinforcing the separation between the inside and the outside.

LB: Yes, definitely, once we're in,

we're really in, like sort of everything's shut outside us. I mean we're eleven storeys up, we can look down on everything and like say, 'We're quite safe, feel quite safe from this position,' and the more we do to it the more it almost seems like a classic escape but, I don't know, it's just an environment where I can feel really happy to be in, like, helps me, my ideas keep ticking over, and I want to work here and keep doing things.

SW: You don't feel like physically distant from the ground or anything like that?

LB: Sometimes like, when I was painting the windows I opened it up and I looked down, it was broad daylight I mean it's eleven storeys up, it's a really long distance and when we first got here we were out on the balcony and we were spitting to see how long it would take to get down,

sort of, like get an idea of it, the distance, it is a long way up, but it's more comforting than disturbing.

SW: What pressures do you kind of . . . ?

LB: Well, sort of, like I've never got enough money to do all the things I want to do, but that's good in a way because I actually become resourceful, I mean, for example that shag pile, we're going to replace it with even better, like this beautiful fun fur, so I mean, yes, being resourceful isn't about, it keeps you like, at your wit's end.

SW: One of the things that interested me was whether you felt that like these days really the only way to get a place like you've got is to do something fairly desperate so that, the only way you can get something out of the council.

LB: I suppose you do get it if you're prepared to wait, but we weren't, we just wanted it straightaway, I mean, we're always a bit sort of eager to get things done like red tape and things like that is pointless so we just tried to think of the fastest way we could, like burning our front door down and pretending we were being harassed all the time, we did that.

SW: Do you find the outside is threatening in some sort of way, I mean when you look out of the window, do you?

LB: Well, when you're on the eleventh floor it's like looking at things through a microscope or sort of above and it doesn't seem like a threat or it seems like you're completely separate, like lifted above it or, so it doesn't sort of bother me, and I never think of it, in the lifts downstairs seem the same as up here, it's a different building outside, up here.

SW: What, even when you just get in your front door?

LB: Yes, it seems like the lift transports us into where we're safe again, where we're happy again.

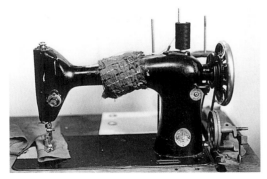

"Every Day and Every Night". March/October 84.
Two panel work, each panel 136 cm x 98cm.

Top left: "Transformers"
Middlesborough. 96/97.
The artist working with
participants, Parliament Road.

Top right: North Peckham Estate,
talking to Mothers and Toddlers
Clubs,"changing Everything'.

Other photographs include: Filming
and participants working on the content
for their Mosaic, at Peckham Library,
Peckham Hill Street.